DARN GOOD ADVICE

Publications International, Ltd.

Contributing writers: Elisabeth Andrews, Jim Daley, Jonathan Kelly, Nina Konrad and Marty Strasen

Images: Wikimedia Commons

Louis Weber, CEO
Publications International, Ltd.
8140 Lehigh Avenue
Morton Grove, IL 60053

ISBN: 978-1-64030-406-2

Manufactured in Canada.

8 7 6 5 4 3 2 1

Introduction

Darn Good Advice is a directory of pragmatic (and sometimes enigmatic) adivce that can help give you guidance when life seems a bit more confounding than usual. Culled from the greatest minds in history, there is no better source to use to help keep your life's trajectory on the right track. Read about the work and lives of earth-moving historical figures. And learn of the trials and tribulations they endured following what they believed.

In the pages that follow, you can find advice from and the bios of culture-changing scientists, writers, politicians, public figures, and others alphabetized by last name. Learn what the famous philosopher Hegel had to say about boundaries, and how his writing has continued to break the boundaries of philosophy nearly a century after his death. See how Gandhi succeeded in attaining Indian independence from the British by following his own advice. Or how Samuel Gompers had a similar piece of advice that he used to accomplish his own goals for the working class of America. These pieces of advice aren't just to help you feel better about yourself, but to kick you into gear to do the right thing.

From the sages of ancient Asia to the Founding Fathers, and from the ancient Greek philosophers to the mavens of the Industrial Revolution, *Darn Good Advice* addresses the ethical, practical, and existential dilemmas that have plagued humanity for millennia. It confronts these dilemmas with deeply contemplated views that can give you a bit of clarity for any situation you might find yourself in. *Darn Good Advice* is packed full of advice that even a trusted mentor would have trouble conjuring. So dive in and begin learning from the greats.

"*Great difficulties may be surmounted by patience and perseverance.*"

A Adams

Adams, Abigail

Wife to one president, mother to another, Abigail Adams was the first First Lady to live in the White House, a prolific letter writer, and a thoughtful analyst of American politics.

Abigail Adams was born Abigail Smith in November 1744, daughter of a minister. Though she did not receive a formal education, she and her sisters read widely, which developed and solidified her formidable intellect.

John and Abigail met when she was seventeen and married a few years later. Their marriage was a close one. During the times when he was away due to business, politics, or war, she handled matters on the home front, and they corresponded frequently, leaving behind a large body of letters that cover a wide array of topics, from family life to politics to the revolution. They wrote over a thousand letters to each other. Adams greatly valued her opinions—though the fledgling republic did not heed Abigail's pleas to "remember the ladies" and grant them more education, independence, and property rights. Their letters provide historians a valuable look at the Revolution, and at the home front during the war. Abigail often signed her letters, "Portia," the name of the wife of the Roman politician Brutus.

During Adams' years in the presidency, Abigail was his hostess, first in Philadelphia and later in D.C., in the newly built White House. She continued to be one of her husband's greatest supporters and an influential advisor—so much so that her opponents derisively dubbed her "Mrs. President."

The presidency of John Adams had its controversies, especially the passage of the Alien and Sedition Acts. Adams lost the presidency to Thomas Jefferson in his bid for re-election. They retired to their home in Massachusetts. Abigail passed away in 1818.

More Quotes From Abigail Adams

"We have too many high sounding words, and too few actions that correspond with them."

"I wish most sincerely there was not a slave in this province. It always appeared a most iniquitous scheme to me—to fight ourselves for what we are daily robbing and plundering from those who have as good a right to freedom as we have."

"I long to hear that you have declared an independency."

"To be good, and to do good, is the whole duty of man comprised in a few words."

"Remember the Ladies, and be more generous and favourable to them than your ancestors."

> *Life cannot be administered by definite rules and regulations; that wisdom to deal with a man's difficulties comes only through some knowledge of his life and habits as a whole . . .*

Jane Addams

Addams, Jane

Jane Addams was a social reformer, feminist and pacifist who founded Hull House, one of the first settlement houses in America in 1889. She was the first female president of the National Conference of Social Work, and won the Nobel Peace Prize in 1931.

Jane Addams was born in Cedarville, Illinois, on September 6, 1860. Her father was a businessman and Illinois State Senator, and was personal friends with Abraham Lincoln. As a child, Addams suffered from tuberculosis that left her with a curved spine, which made it difficult for her to play with other children. She would have lifelong health problems as a result. As a teenager, she read Charles Dickens, and his books inspired a desire to work among the poor. She studied at Rockford Female Seminary, graduating in 1881. That same year her

father died, and she inherited $50,000 (about $1.2 million today). Addams attended medical school in Philadelphia, but illness prevented her from completing her degree. In 1887 she travelled with her close friend Ellen Gates Starr to London, where she visited Toynbee Hall. Toynbee was a settlement house; these establishments brought middle-class volunteers to live and work among the poor, providing day care, education, and healthcare. Addams and Starr resolved to start a settlement house in Chicago.

Hull House

In 1889 Addams and Starr opened Hull House on Chicago's near west side. It was one of the first settlement houses in North America. The settlement was named for the building's original owner, and Addams and Starr organized it to provide services to immigrants and poor residents of the surrounding tenements. The organization eventually grew to more than ten buildings. Hull House provided child care, a public kitchen, educational classes, an art gallery, a summer camp, and social programs. Hull House built the first public playground in the city, and established a theater group that has been credited as the founder of the American "Little Theater" Movement.

Addams and Starr also provided emergency medical services when doctors were not available, often volunteering as midwives and nurses. Hull House also was one of the first organizations that sheltered victims of domestic violence. Hull House advocated for the people it served, leading efforts to pass legislation at all levels of government on child welfare, women's suffrage and healthcare and immigration reform.

Other Work

Addams served on the Chicago Board of Education beginning in 1905, chairing the Board's School Management Committee. In 1910 she was elected the first female president of the National Conference of Social Work, and the next year she established the National Federation of Settlements, which she led for more than twenty years. At the outbreak of World War I, Addams became the chair of the Women's Peace Party, and spoke regularly on pacifism. In 1915 she attended the International Congress of Women at the Hague with social reformers Emily Greene Balch and Alice Hamilton. From 1919 to 1929 she was president of the International Committee of Women for a Permanent Peace. She shared the Nobel Peace Prize in 1931 for her work promoting pacifism.

Many of the Hull House buildings were torn down when the University of Illinois at Chicago was built in 1963. The original Hull House remains on Halsted Avenue on the near west side, and is now a museum. Jane Addams died on May 21, 1935, in Chicago, Illinois.

More Quotes From Jane Addams

"What after all, has maintained the human race on this old globe despite all the calamities of nature and all the tragic failings of mankind, if not faith in new possibilities, and courage to advocate them."

"Civilization is a method of living, an attitude of equal respect for all men."

"In his own way each man must struggle, lest the moral law become a far-off abstraction utterly separated from his active life."

"Of all the aspects of social misery nothing is so heartbreaking as unemployment ..."

"Hospitality still survives among foreigners, although it is buried under false pride among the poorest Americans."

> *Resolved to take Fate by the throat and shake a living out of her.*

L. M. Alcott

Alcott, Louisa May

Louisa May Alcott was a prolific writer whose novel *Little Women*, loosely based on her and her sisters' upbringing, has become one of the classics of American literature.

Louisa May Alcott was born on November 29, 1832, in the Germantown section of Philadelphia. Her father, Bronson Alcott, was a teacher and her mother, Abby May, was a social worker. Bronson Alcott was a transcendentalist, and Louisa grew up among leaders of that movement, including Ralph Waldo Emerson and Henry David Thoreau. Alcott was educated primarily by her father, who ran an experimental school in Boston; she attended it for some time and was also educated at home. While her father had altruistic ideals, his transcendentalist utopian community, The Fruitlands, was a failure, and her family struggled to make ends meet. (Alcott wrote at one point, "My definition [of a philosopher] is of a man up in a balloon, with his family and friends holding the ropes which confine him to earth and trying to haul him down.") Alcott worked as a teacher, seamstress, and domestic servant to help support her family. Writing soon became a creative outlet for Alcott. Her first book, *Flower Fables*, a collection of short stories she had originally written for Ralph Waldo Emerson's daughter, was published when she was seventeen.

The Civil War and *Little Women*

Alcott was raised in a socially progressive environment. Her parents, like almost all transcendentalists, were opposed to slavery. In 1847 her home became a station on the Underground

Railroad when her family housed a fugitive slave for one week. Alcott read the Seneca Falls Declaration of Sentiments in 1848, and became the first woman to register to vote in Concord, Massachusetts. Her writing reflected her feminist ideas, depicting imaginative, self-reliant female protagonists, who, like Alcott herself, had to shake a living out of Fate. When the Civil War broke out, she volunteered as a nurse, but contracted typhoid and had to return home. In 1863 she wrote of her experiences in *Hospital Sketches*, which brought her acclaim. She began writing stories for *The Atlantic Monthly*. In 1868 she wrote *Little Women* in part to help support her family financially.

Little Women tells the story of four sisters, Meg, Jo, Beth, and Amy March, and is largely based on recollections of Alcott's own childhood. The character Jo is based on Alcott. The sisters' New England family is not affluent, but has a generally optimistic view of life. The book follows the sisters as they grow up and grapple with the challenges of adult life, including employment and marriage. The book was immediately successful, and allowed Alcott to settle her family's debts. In 1870 Alcott embarked on a European tour to promote the book, which was published as *Good Wives* in the United Kingdom. She followed it with two sequels: *Little Men* in 1871 and *Jo's Boys* in 1886. She also wrote eleven unrelated novels under her own name and four more under a pseudonym. She published a collection of short stories in six volumes between 1872–1882.

Other than her trip to Europe and occasional visits to New York City, Alcott spent the remained of her life between Boston and Concord. She never married, and cared for her parents. Late in life, she adopted her niece, also named Louisa May after her. Her mother died after a long illness in 1877, and her father died ten years later. Alcott died on March 6, 1888, in Boston.

She is buried in Sleepy Hollow Cemetery in Boston, on a hillside known as Authors' Ridge, where Nathaniel Hawthorne, Emerson, and Henry David Thoreau are also buried.

More Quotes From Louisa May Alcott

"Women have been called queens for a long time, but the kingdom given them isn't worth ruling."

"I believe that it is as much a right and duty for women to do something with their lives as for men and we are not going to be satisfied with such frivolous parts as you give us."

"Far away in the sunshine are my highest aspirations. I may not reach them, but I can look up and see their beauty, believe in them, and try to follow where they lead."

"I am angry nearly every day of my life, but I have learned not to show it; and I still try to hope not to feel it, though it may take me another forty years to do it."

> *For the things we have to learn before we can do, we learn by doing.*
>
> —Aristotle

Aristotle

Aristotle's impact on Western knowledge was incredibly profound. He is widely regarded as creating the earliest known comprehensive system of Western philosophy, with contributions to physics, biology, logic, ethics, government, and the arts. His shift from Platonism, which argued for the coexistence of a *perceptible* reality and an *imperceptible* one, to Empiricism, which holds that human knowledge is rooted in that which can be observed, was nothing short of revolutionary in its influence.

Born in Greece in 384 BCE, Aristotle joined Plato's Academy in Athens when he was a teenager, and studied there for the next twenty years of his life. While there, he immersed himself in Platonic thought and scientific study.

Following the death of Plato in 347 BCE, Aristotle left Athens to become the head of the Royal Academy of Macedon. He was the royal tutor to Alexander the Great and other future Macedonian kings. His position as Alexander's tutor allowed him to influence world politics at the time: he personally encouraged Alexander to invade Persia and pursue his conquest of Asia Minor. His position also gave him the resources necessary to establish his own school, the Lyceum, where he completed many of his most influential writings.

Some of his most influential works include *Physics, Metaphysics, On the Soul*, and *Poetics*. Aristotle's wide-ranging studies are generally considered to be not only an index of

Greek knowledge at the time, but also constitute the foundation of Western thought for the next two millennia.

After Alexander died in 323 BCE, growing anti-Macedonian sentiment in Athens forced Aristotle to flee. Upon leaving, he declared, "I will not allow the Athenians to sin twice against Philosophy," referring to the execution of Socrates in Athens in 399 BCE. Aristotle died later that year.

More Quotes From Aristotle

"Knowledge of the fact differs from knowledge of the reason for the fact."

"We should venture on the study of every kind of animal without distaste; for each and all will reveal to us something natural and something beautiful."

"Piety requires us to honor truth above our friends."

"One swallow does not a summer make."

"Any one can get angry—that is easy—or give or spend money; but to do this to the right person, to the right extent, at the right time, with the right motive, and in the right way, that is not for every one, nor is it easy."

> # *The more a man judges, the less he loves.*

Balzac, Honoré de

French writer Honoré de Balzac wrote of life, influenced Realism, and had an interesting love life that could be a great piece of literature all its own.

Honoré de Balzac was born in France in 1799. A prolific novelist, playwright, and essayist, he was an early writer in the Realism movement, trying to depict humans as fascinating, dynamic, and sometimes flawed individuals. His magnum opus, *La Comedie Humaine*, was a series of linked novels, stories, and essays depicting French life and society.

Balzac's own marriage could come from a story. He entered into a correspondence with a woman who wrote him a letter in response to one of his works. The first letter was sent anonymously, but it so intrigued Balzac that he put out an advertisement to try to encourage the writer to contact him again—sort of an early version of Craiglist's Missed Connections! The writer, a married Polish noblewoman named Ewelina Hańska, did respond, and they began a correspondence that would last fifteen years. After Hańska was widowed in 1841, she and Balzac pursued a romantic relationship. The road to marriage was circuitous due to financial setbacks and various objections from outside. In 1850, the couple married. Balzac, in poor health, died only five months later. Victor Hugo acted as the eulogist at his funeral. Balzac left behind a rich legacy of works, a number of unfinished and planned works, and a fascinating life story.

More Quotes From Balzac

"Marriage is a fight to the death, before which the wedded couple ask a blessing from heaven, because it is the rashest of all undertakings to swear eternal love; the fight at once commences and victory, that is to say liberty, remains in the hands of the cleverer of the two."

"The most virtuous women have in them something that is never chaste."

"Love is the most melodious of all harmonies and the sentiment of love is innate."

"Our heart is a treasury; if you pour out all its wealth at once, you are bankrupt. We show no more mercy to the affection that reveals its utmost extent than we do to another kind of prodigal who has not a penny left."

"Love has its own instinct, finding the way to the heart, as the feeblest insect finds the way to its flower, with a will which nothing can dismay nor turn aside."

> *Seek not the paths of the ancients; Seek that which the ancients sought.*
>
> —Matsuo Basho

Basho, Matsuo

"My poetry is like a stove in the summer or a fan in the winter. It runs against the popular tastes and has no practical use." So said Matsuo Basho—but he was perceived by others as a master of the art with a profound insight into life and nature.

Matsuo Basho did not invent the haiku, though he did become a master of the art. In fact, the form of poetry was not called haiku in his day, but rather *hokku*. Basho, born near Ueno in 1644, was the only one of his siblings to show an interest in literature over farming. He moved to Kyoto and began studying Chinese poetry and Taoism under a well-respected local poet. Basho began writing in a style called *haikai no renga*. It was a style constructed in a series of related verses, the opening verse known as *hokku*.

Writers soon began composing these three-line verses— consisting of five, seven, and five syllables, and frequently calling on imagery from nature—as standalone poems. Basho mastered the style that would come to be called haiku. He published several under different names until 1680, when a student gave him basho trees as a gift. Thereafter, he was Basho.

Trials shaped his life and his writings. A fire that destroyed his home and most of his city in the early 1680s may have contributed to a period in his life when he shut himself off from the world and remained in a hut. However, he embraced Buddhist philosophies and eventually made a conscious decision to embrace the world around him, rather than shunning it. Many of his best writings came from his subsequent travel.

The Long Road

Though Basho wrote many of his poems in what is now Tokyo, it was a journey he took on foot in 1689 that led to his most famous work, *Oku no Hosomichi*, or *Narrow Road to the Interior*. Before the journey, he had created his own form of poetry called *haibun*. It was a hybrid style that combined haiku with prose and was perfect for chronicling a progression or journey. That's precisely what Basho set out on.

Over a five-month span of 1689, Basho and his apprentice, Sora, traveled 1,200 miles on foot. They headed north from Tokyo, through the uplands and lowlands of the northern province of Tohuku, and then southwest along the Sea of Japan to the central city of Ogaki. It was a journey that inspired his greatest writings, and one that his disciples follow still today in an effort to walk in his footsteps.

Every year thousands of people make pilgrimages to Basho's Trail, his birthplace, and to his burial shrine. A linguist born and raised in Kyoto, the late Helen Tanizaki, once said, "Everyone I went to school with could recite at least one of Basho's poems by heart. He was the first writer we read in any exciting or serious way."

Basho's Legacy

Though he was certainly respected in his time as a beautiful poet for his simple and natural style, Basho gained even wider acclaim after his death at age fifty. Recall that haiku was not a widespread form at the time. Throughout the eighteenth century, he was celebrated as a pioneer of the haiku form that became revered for its beauty.

His works became widely translated in the 1900s, when his influence continued to climb. He was an inspiration to American writers like Ezra Pound and even many U.S. Beat Generation poets in the 1950s and '60s for his simplicity and use of imagery and embracing of the world around him.

More Quotes From Matsuo Basho

"Every day is a journey, and the journey itself is home."

"There is nothing you can see that is not a flower; / There is nothing you can think that is not the moon."

"Who mourns makes grief his master. / Who drinks makes pleasure his master."

"The haiku that reveals seventy to eighty percent of its subject is good. Those that reveal fifty to sixty percent, we never tire of."

"He who creates three to five haiku poems during a lifetime is a haiku poet. He who attains to complete ten is a master."

If you would be accounted great by your contemporaries, be not too much greater than they.

Ambrose Bierce

Bierce, Ambrose

American journalist, satirist, and author, Ambrose Bierce is famous for his short story "An Occurrence at Owl Creek Bridge" and *The Devil's Dictionary*, in which he redefines a number of words in the distinct tone of his irreverent humor.

Ambrose Gwinnett Bierce was born on June 24, 1824, in Ohio and grew up in Warsaw, Indiana. After attending high school for only about a year, he began working as a printer's apprentice. When the Civil War broke out in 1861, Bierce joined the 9th Indiana Volunteers and saw action in several major battles, including Shiloh, Chickamauga, and Kennesaw Mountain, where he was severely wounded. He remained in the Army until January 1865 and was eventually promoted to Major.

Life and Career

Following the War, Bierce moved to San Francisco, where he began writing for the *News Letter* and a number of other periodicals in 1867. He began editing the *News Letter* the following year, and his reputation soon spread all over the West Coast. He published his first short story, "The Haunted Valley," in 1871, and on Christmas Day of that year he married Mary Ellen Day. In 1872 the couple moved to London, where they lived for the next three years. While they were there, Bierce began contributing humorous and satirical pieces to magazines such as *Figaro* and *Fun*, and edited the *Lantern*. In 1873 he published a collection of the articles he wrote in London in *The Fiend's Delight*, and published *Nuggets and Dust Panned Out in California* in 1872 and *Cobwebs from an Empty Skull* in 1874.

Bierce and his wife returned to San Francisco in 1875, and in 1877 he began editing the *Argonaut*. After a brief stint as a local manager for a mining company in the Dakota Territory, he returned to San Francisco again, and in 1887 became a staff writer for the *San Francisco Examiner*, a newspaper published by William Randolph Hearst. He would continue to write for Hearst newspapers until 1909. In 1888 Bierce discovered a cache of letters written to his wife by an admirer, and they separated, divorcing in 1904. Bierce left San Francisco in 1896, moving to Washington, D.C., where he continued to contribute to newspapers and magazines on the East Coast. In October 1913 he travelled to Mexico, which at the time was in the turmoil of Pancho Villa's revolution. He joined Villa's army as an observer, and disappeared sometime after December 26. The date and circumstances of his death remain a mystery.

Literary Legacy

Bierce's principal work of fiction is *In the Midst of Life*, published in 1892. It includes the famous short stories "The Boarded Window," "A Horseman in the Sky," and "An Occurrence at Owl Creek Bridge." "Occurrence," which first appeared in the *San Francisco Examiner* and was also published in *Tales of Soldiers and Civilians*, is notable for its nonlinear timeline, twist ending, and use of stream of consciousness. The story has been adapted numerous times and influenced many later works that used a similar surprise twist ending.

The Devil's Dictionary, which Bierce wrote in a series of installments in magazines and newspapers over three decades beginning in 1867, is a collection of satirical definitions published in 1911. Bierce had begun including satirical definitions from time to time in his early essays, and published his first essay with multiple satirical definitions in *Webster Revisited* in 1869. He began working on the dictionary in earnest in 1875. Although critical reception was initially mixed, it has since come to be considered one of the greatest satirical works in American literature.

It is not known when or where Bierce died exactly. The last correspondence from him came from Chihuahua, Mexico, where he was gaining first hand experience in the Mexican Revolution in 1914. He was never heard from again.

Definitions From Ambrose Bierce

"Abnormal, adj. Not conforming to standards in matters of thought and conduct. To be independent is to be abnormal, to be abnormal is to be detested."

"Absurdity, n. A statement or belief manifestly inconsistent with one's own opinion."

"Alone, adj. In bad company."

"Birth, n. The first and direst of all disasters."

"Bore, n. A person who talks when you wish him to listen."

"Conservative, n. A statesman enamored of existing evils, as opposed to a Liberal, who wants to replace them with others."

"Dictionary, n. A malevolent literary device for cramping the growth of a language and making it hard and inelastic. This dictionary, however, is a most useful work."

"Education, n. That which discloses to the wise and disguises from the foolish their lack of understanding."

"Heaven, n. A place where the wicked cease from troubling you with talk of their personal affairs, and the good listen with attention while you expound your own."

"Laughter, n. An interior convulsion, producing a distortion of the features and accompanied by inarticulate noises. It is infectious and, though intermittent, incurable."

"Neighbor, n. One whom we are commanded to love as ourselves, and who does all he knows how to make us disobedient."

"Philosophy, n. A route of many roads leading from nowhere to nothing."

"Politeness, n. The most acceptable hypocrisy."

"Positive, adj. Mistaken at the top of one's voice."

"Quotation, n. The act of repeating erroneously the words of another. The words erroneously repeated."

"Success, n. The one unpardonable sin against one's fellows."

"Year, n. A period of three hundred and sixty-five disappointments."

> ## *Self-conceit is the enemy of progress.*
> —Bion of Borysthenes

Bion of Borysthenes

His father was a fishmonger and a smuggler, and his mother was a prostitute. The slave of a Greek rhetorician, Bion burned his master's library and gave away his inheritance after his death and fled to Athens, where he became one of the greatest Cynics of the ancient world.

Bion was born around 325 BCE on the coast of the Black Sea to free parents, but because his father was charged with a number of crimes, his family was sold into slavery when he was still a young man. After making his way to Athens, Bion studied at Plato's Academy, traveled extensively throughout Greece and Macedonia, and eventually became a teacher at the Academy in Rhodes.

Unlike other scholars of his day, Bion was not associated with Platonism, instead joining the Cynics of Diogenes and Antisthenes. Cynics believed that the meaning of life was found by living virtuously and in harmony with nature. They lived simply, eschewing worldly goods and attacking social traditions.

Bion was known for his withering attacks on his opponents, who included the gods, musicians, astrologers, the wealthy, and the devout. His most well-known work, *Diatribes*, ruthlessly satirized people's general foolishness and poked fun at the human condition. He advocated using common sense when dealing with life's problems, no matter how big or small—from the fear of death to poverty to exile and slavery. His writings were widely cited by historians, including Plutarch and Cicero.

Bion died sometime around 250 BCE in Chaclis in Euboea.

More Quotes From Bion of Borysthenes

"Though boys throw stones at frogs in sport, the frogs do not die in sport, but in earnest."

"How stupid it was for the king to tear out his hair in grief, as if baldness were a cure for sorrow."

"Old age is the harbor of all ills."

"Love of money is the mother-city of all evils."

"The road to Hades is easy to travel; at any rate men pass away with their eyes shut."

"He has not acquired a fortune; the fortune has acquired him."

"[A]cknowledge no master in human form."

John Brown

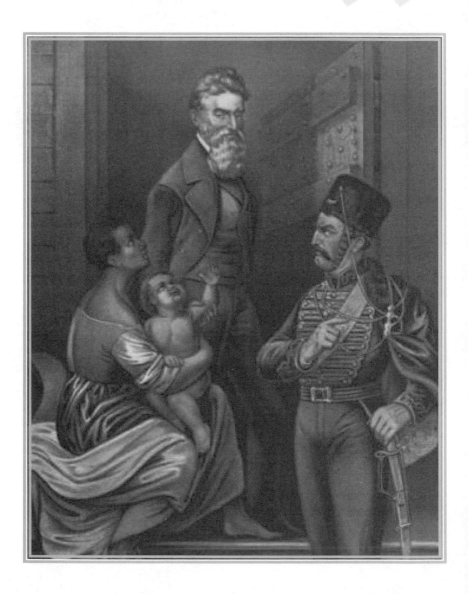

Brown, John

John Brown was a militant abolitionist who participated in the Bloody Kansas conflict and led a raid on Harpers Ferry in an attempt to spark an uprising against slavery in 1859.

John Brown was born on May 9, 1800, in Torrington, Connecticut. His father, a Calvinist minister, taught him at a young age to support abolition. The lesson was seared into Brown's memory when he was twelve years old and witnessed the beating of a young African-American boy. Brown initially studied to be a minister, but instead became a tanner. His family moved around in his twenties and held different jobs.

In 1837, when the abolitionist Elijah Lovejoy was murdered, Brown swore to give his life to the abolitionist cause. He founded the League of Gileadites, an armed group that protected African-Americans from slave catchers. In 1847 he met with Frederick Douglass. When the Kansas-Nebraska Act passed in 1854, Brown and five of his sons moved to Kansas to fight in the conflict over whether the state would be free or slave-owning territory. They killed five pro-slavery settlers in 1856.

In 1858 Brown freed a group of slaves from a Missouri farm and led them to freedom in Canada. He spent much of that year and the spring and summer of 1859 making preparations for the raid on Harpers Ferry. He gathered rifles, pikes, and ammunition and organized a group of twenty-one men. He discussed the raid with Harriet Tubman, who thought it was doomed to failure. On October 16, 1859, Brown and his men attacked the federal armory at Harpers Ferry and held it for two days before they were overwhelmed by federal troops led by Robert E. Lee.

Brown was captured and convicted of treason. On December 2, 1859, he was executed. He became a symbol of the abolitionist movement, and during the Civil War Union troops sang "John Brown's Body" as they marched into battle.

More Quotes From John Brown

"These men are all talk; What is needed is action—action!"

"I am yet too young to understand that God is any respecter of persons. I believe that to have interfered as I have done as I have always freely admitted I have done in behalf of His despised poor, was not wrong, but right. Now, if it is deemed necessary that I should forfeit my life for the furtherance of the ends of justice, and mingle my blood further with the blood of my children and with the blood of millions in this slave country whose rights are disregarded by wicked, cruel, and unjust enactments, I submit; so let it be done!"

Every human being has, like Socrates, an attendant spirit; and wise are they who obey its signals. If it does not always tell us what to do, it always cautions us what not to do.

L. Maria Child.

Child, Lydia Maria

Lydia Maria Child was a writer, antislavery activist, and feminist who wrote a number of abolitionist books that were highly influential in the lead-up to the American Civil War.

Lydia Maria Child (née Francis) was born in Medford, Massachusetts, on February 11, 1802. Her family was Unitarian and staunchly abolitionist. Her brother, a Unitarian minister and a professor at Harvard, was highly influential in her education, and helped expose her to works by Homer and Milton. She became a teacher at the Medford Seminary in 1824, and that year she wrote her first novel, *Hobomok*. In 1826 she founded the *Juvenile Miscellany*, a magazine for children. She married David Child, an editor, in 1828. When she met William Lloyd Garrison in 1831, she dedicated herself to the cause of abolition.

Child published *An Appeal in Favor of That Class of Americans Called Africans* in 1833. The book argued for equality of education and employment for African-Americans. The book was very controversial, and led to her magazine failing in 1834. But it also served to convince many people to join the abolitionist movement. She began editing the *National Anti-Slavery Standard* in 1841. Child and her husband moved to Wayland, Massachusetts, in 1852. There she wrote several more books, including *The Freedmen's Book*, a compilation of the life stories of former slaves, in 1865, and *An Appeal for the Indians*, which called for justice for Native Americans. An Appeal helped encourage the creation of the U.S. Board of

Indian Commissioners and President Grant's adoption of a Peace Policy towards Native Americans.

Despite her long history of advocacy, Child's most familiar words to us today are probably from her poetry for children; she was the writer of "Over the river and through the wood, to grandfather's house we go."

Lydia Maria Child died October 20, 1880, at her home in Wayland.

More Quotes From Lydia Maria Child

"We first crush people to the earth, and then claim the right of trampling on them forever, because they are prostrate."

"They [the slaves] have stabbed themselves for freedom—jumped into the waves for freedom—starved for freedom—fought like very tigers for freedom! But they have been hung, and burned, and shot—and their tyrants have been their historians!"

"I think we have reason to thank God for Abraham Lincoln. With all his deficiencies, it must be admitted that he has grown continually."

"Yours for the unshackled exercise of every faculty by every human being."

> *Learning without thought is naught; thought without learning is dangerous.*
>
> —Confucius

像教行子孔師先

Confucius

Born Kong Qui in the Lu state of China during the Spring and Autumn Period of Chinese history, Confucius developed a system of teachings around ethics, family, and education that would become the official imperial philosophy of China for centuries. His work was particularly influential during the Han, Tang, and Song dynasties.

Confucius was born circa 551 BCE in the present-day Shandong Province in China. Very little is known of his early life, and accounts vary so widely that some claim he was born into poverty while others assert he was raised as part of a royal family of the Chou Dynasty.

During his life, several rival Chinese states were competing with the Chou Dynasty, which at the time had ruled for more than five centuries. The resulting turmoil undermined traditional Chinese principles and led to a period of moral decline. Confucius seized upon this opportunity to begin spreading teachings that were focused on restoring traditional values based around compassion. His philosophy was couched in the simple idea called *ren*. The idea includes the dual tenets of loving others and practicing self-discipline in what was perhaps the earliest recorded instance of the Golden Rule.

With regard to family, he advocated for family loyalty, ancestor veneration, and respect of elders by children and wives by husbands.

The concept of self-discipline also infused Confucius' political philosophy. He taught that leaders had to exercise self-discipline so that they could lead by a positive example, treating their followers with respect and compassion while remaining humble in their position of power. Confucius taught that leaders could inspire their subjects to respect the rule of law by teaching them to be virtuous and unite using ritual decorum and good manners.

Confucius promoted a philosophy of education based on the Six Arts of archery, calligraphy, chariot-driving, mathematics, music, and ritual. He believed that the main purpose of education was to teach the people to lead lives of integrity and honor. He attempted to restore the traditional values of generosity, respectability, and ritual in Chinese society through his educational philosophy.

Major Writings

Many of the most influential works of classical Chinese writing including all of the Five Classics were written or edited by Confucius. Among others, he revised the *Book of Odes* and the *Book of Documents,* a classic historical work on ancient China. He also wrote a history of the nobles of Lu, a vassal state during the Zhou dynasty, called *The Spring and Autumn Annals.*

Confucius' political and philosophical beliefs are collected in the *Lunyu*, which may have been composed by his disciples. It is one of the Four Books that were published by Zhu Xi in 1190 CE, and that make up the core of Confucianism. *Lunyu* was translated into English as *The Analects of Confucius*.

Confucius died in Qufu in 479 BCE, a year after his son Tzu-lu was killed in battle. At the time of his death, he believed his teachings had had no real impact on Chinese culture or society, but by the fourth century BCE, he had become widely regarded as a brilliant philosopher and sage who had not received the proper recognition during his life. During the Han Dynasty in the second century BCE, Confucius' philosophy had become the foundation of the official state ideology, and he remains one of the most influential thinkers in Chinese history.

More Quotes From Confucius

"To learn and then do, is not that a pleasure? When friends come from afar do we not rejoice? To live unknown and not fret, is not that to be a gentleman?"

"Smooth words and fawning looks are seldom found with love."

"The young should be dutiful at home, modest abroad, careful and true, overflowing in kindness for all, but in brotherhood with love. And if they have strength to spare they should spend it on the arts."

"He that rules by mind is like the north star, steady in his seat, whilst the stars all bend to him."

"The three hundred poems are summed up in the one line, Think no evil."

"Lift up the straight, put away the crooked; and the people will be won. Lift up the crooked, put away the straight; and the people will not be won."

"A man without love, what is courtesy to him? A man without love, what is music to him?"

"Loveless men cannot bear need long, they cannot bear fortune long. Loving men find peace in love, the wise find profit in it."

"Whilst thy father and mother are living, do not wander afar. If thou must travel, hold a set course."

"We shall seldom get lost if we hold to main lines."

"A great soul is never friendless: he has always neighbours."

"Love is to conquer self and turn to courtesy. If we could conquer self and turn to courtesy for one day, all below heaven would turn to love. Does love flow from within, or does it flow from others?"

"Rank thy work above success, will not the mind be raised? Fight the bad in thee, not the bad in other men, will not evil be mended?"

"If good men were to govern a land for an hundred years, cruelty would be conquered and putting to death done away with."

"What is governing to a man that can rule himself? If he cannot rule himself, how shall he rule others?"

"Woe to the man whose heart has not learned while young to hope, to love—and to put its trust in life!!

Joseph Conrad

Conrad, Joseph

Joseph Conrad's novels *Lord Jim*, *Heart of Darkness*, and *The Secret Agent*, explored the darker aspects of human nature and were loosely based on his own travels in South America, Asia, and Africa.

Joseph Conrad (Jozef Konrad Korzeniowski) was born in Berdychiv, Ukraine, on December 3, 1857. His parents were members of the Polish aristocracy, and supported the Polish independence movement against Russian rule. When he was four years old, Conrad's parents were arrested for their patriotic activities and sent to Vologda in northwest Russia. They died a few years later, and Conrad returned to Poland, where he was raised by an uncle. As a child, Conrad was tutored at home by his father, and upon his return to Poland he attended school in Krakow.

When he was sixteen years old, he travelled to Marseilles, France, where found work on merchant ships. He traveled to South America and served as a ship's apprentice and ship's steward, and may have taken part in international gun-running. In his twenties, following a failed suicide attempt due to debts, he joined the British Merchant Navy, where he served for sixteen years. During his time as a merchant marine, Conrad sailed around the world, traveling to India, Singapore, Australia, and Africa. He was promoted multiple times and granted British citizenship.

Literary Career

Conrad began working on his first novel, *Almayer's Folly*, while he was in the Merchant Navy. The book is an adventure tale set in the jungles of Borneo. When he left the seafaring life in 1894, it was for several reasons, but his desire to begin a literary career was chief among them. He published *Almayer's* in 1895, and it received mixed reactions from critics due to the author's clear awkwardness with the English language. In 1896 he published *An Outpost of Progress*, a short story set in Belgium-controlled Congo, and *An Outcast of the Islands*, a novel set in Indonesia. Like his later novels, *Outpost* and *Outcast* were both critical of colonialism. Conrad married Jessie Emmeline George in 1896, and the couple had two children.

In 1900 Conrad published *Lord Jim* to critical acclaim. The book tells the story of a young sailor who, with his fellow crewmen, abandoned his ship while it was in distress, leaving the passengers to drown. The passengers are rescued, however, and Jim must grapple with the consequences of his cowardice. He travels to the South Pacific and eventually becomes the leader of a small country there.

In 1902 Conrad published what is perhaps his most famous novel, *Heart of Darkness*. Like *Outpost*, it is set in the Belgian Congo. The protagonist, an Englishman named Marlow, travels up the Congo River where he encounters a brutal and mysterious ivory trader named Kurtz, who has made himself the ruler of the native people in his area. *Heart of Darkness* examines the cruelty of humankind, and compares the "darkness" of both London and the Congo, arguing that civilized people have much in common with those they describe as "savage." The book is highly critical of colonial practices, which Conrad was familiar with from his years as a seafarer, and contains the lines, "The horror! The horror!" that have been referenced by multiple works through the decades that have followed, often in parody.

He died in Canterbury, England, on August 3, 1924.

More Quotes From Joseph Conrad

"It's only those who do nothing that make no mistakes, I suppose."

"It is to be remarked that a good many people are born curiously unfitted for the fate awaiting them on this earth."

"Being a woman is a terribly difficult trade since it consists principally of dealings with men."

"In plucking the fruit of memory one runs the risk of spoiling its bloom."

"A man is a worker. If he is not that he is nothing."

"*As for a future life, every man must judge for himself between conflicting vague probabilities.*"

Charles Darwin

Darwin, Charles

Charles Darwin is one of the greatest biologists in history. He himself took a chance on his own wild theory by betting that life had developed its great variability from vague probabilities and chance mutations. His breakthrough insight that natural selection is the driver of evolution revolutionized biology and directly led to every major advance in the life sciences since he described it in *On the Origin of Species*.

Darwin was born to a scientific family on February 12, 1809. His father Robert was a physician, and his grandfather Erasmus had theorized on evolution and the possibility of a single common ancestor for all his life. Darwin was a capable student, but he preferred taking long walks in the countryside to the classroom. At sixteen he attended medical school, but disliked the curriculum, although he enjoyed chemistry and zoology. He left medical school and enrolled in Cambridge in 1828, where he continued to pursue zoology, collecting beetles in his spare time.

The Voyage of the *Beagle*

After completing Cambridge, Darwin was offered a position as a naturalist on the HMS *Beagle*, a survey ship that would take a five-year voyage around the Southern Hemisphere. It was on this voyage that Darwin had his first inklings of what would become the Theory of Natural Selection. At Cape Verde, he observed ancient seashells on high cliffs far from the water. The ship's captain lent Darwin a copy of Charles Lyell's *Principles of*

Geology, which argued that geologic change was the result of continual accumulation of minuscule changes over time.

In the Galapagos Islands, Darwin observed variations among tortoise shells from one island to the next, and saw that a number of similar finches had very different beaks that appeared related to their diet. The Galapagos animals were also clearly related to South American species, but had small differences. These observations laid the foundation for his discovery of natural selection.

On the Origin of Species

Darwin would spend the next twenty years variously presenting his findings from the voyage, writing books on geology, and assembling a comprehensive classification of barnacles. All the while, he was quietly writing about his theories on natural selection, but kept his discovery to himself; he was aware of the radical implications of the theory, and wanted to be absolutely certain it was airtight.

In 1858, however, his hand was forced when he received a letter from Alfred Russell Wallace describing his own very similar theories on natural selection. Their theories were jointly presented at the Linnaean Society on July 1, and in November 1859, Darwin's *On the Origin of Species* was published. The first printing of 1,250 copies sold out almost immediately, and the book sparked international interest. The *Origin* argued that all extant life on earth arose from a single common ancestor, that many more offspring are produced than can survive, and that slight variations among those offspring will allow some to have a better chance at survival.

Darwin eventually published six editions of the *Origin of Species*; many of the ideas associated with it, such as "survival of the fittest," did not appear until later editions; the word "evolved" appears only once in the first edition, and "evolution" was not added until the fifth. Although the theory was resisted by a few members of the scientific elite and the Church of England, the evidence for it was irrefutable, and it was soon widely accepted as fact. Darwin continued his work after the publication, writing two books on botany. In 1871 he published *The Descent of Man* and *Selection in Relation to Sex*, which demonstrated that humans are animals and laid out his theory of evolution by sexual selection.

Darwin died in 1882, and was buried in Westminster Abbey.

No man can tell what the future may bring forth, and small opportunities are often the beginning of great enterprises.

—Demosthenes

Demosthenes

Demosthenes, born in Athens in 384 BCE, was considered the greatest of the Greek orators, and is famous for having incited the Athenians to fight against Phillip of Macedonia as well as Phillip's son Alexander the Great.

Demosthenes' first taste of oratory came at the age of twenty, when he successfully argued to gain the remainder of his family inheritance from his appointed guardians. For a number of years Demosthenes worked in the law and wrote speeches for lawsuits.

In his thirties, Demosthenes began to speak publicly; this is when he first began his political rhetoric. To strengthen his voice, he practiced speaking over the roar of waves at the coast with his mouth full of pebbles. Demosthenes' oratory was convincing: following the death of Phillip, he helped incite a rebellion against Alexander in 335 BCE. The rebellion was crushed, however, and while Demosthenes was spared, he'd become a marked man in the eyes of the Macedonians.

The following year, a number of Demosthenes' admirers in Athens suggested that the city honor him for his speeches by presenting him with a crown. The idea quickly became a political issue, and in 330 BCE, one of his supporters, Ctesiphon, was prosecuted for proposing the idea. In what became his most famous speech, "On the Crown," Demosthenes attacked his political opponents and convinced them to release Ctesiphon.

When Alexander died, Demosthenes began to urge another revolt, but Alexander's successor quickly subdued the Athenians and condemned him and other rebels to death. Rather than be captured, Demosthenes took his own life on October 12, 322 BCE. He was 62 years old.

More Quotes From Demosthenes

"Nothing is easier than self-deceit. For what each man wishes, that he also believes to be true."

"It is not possible to found a lasting power upon injustice, perjury, and treachery."

"Every advantage in the past is judged in the light of the final issue."

"The readiest and surest way to get rid of censure, is to correct ourselves."

> *In order to seek truth, it is necessary once in the course of our life, to doubt, as far as possible, of all things.*
>
> —Descartes

Descartes, René

A mathematician, philosopher, and scientist, Descartes almost single-handedly invented modern Western philosophy.

René Descartes was born in a small town in central France on March 31, 1596; the town has since been named after him. He was raised by his maternal grandmother until he was eight years old, when he was sent to a Jesuit boarding school until he was fifteen. There, he studied rhetoric, natural philosophy, ethics, and astronomy. He attended the University of Poitiers, where he studied law. He is widely credited with being the architect of modern Western philosophy; his ideas were radical for their time. Descartes believed that all ideas that preceded him should be cleared away, as they were preconceived and inherited. Instead, he declared the starting place for determining the new philosophy to be simply the statement "I exist." From this statement he deduced the quote he is most famous for: I think, therefore I am. (In Latin, *Cogito, ergo sum*; in French, *Je pense, donc je suis.*)

In saying so, he echoed St. Augustine, 1,200 years earlier: "Of this last doubt, I cannot doubt: that I doubt," and an even earlier statement by Aristotle: "To be conscious that we are perceiving or thinking is to be conscious of our own existence." Neither of those fit so easily on a T-shirt, though!

Descartes contended that all truths—natural, philosophical physical, and metaphysical—were ultimately linked as parts of a greater, complete Truth. This was, to some degree, an extension of the ideas that had been proposed by Frances Bacon early on in the seventeenth century. Descartes' most famous treatises are perhaps *Meditations on First Philosophy* and *Principles of Philosophy*, in which he developed many of the ideas he would become famous for. These works continue to be standards in philosophy studies the world over. He also developed the Cartesian coordinate system of geometry, which is still used today and is the foundation of much of modern mathematics.

Descartes died on February 11, 1650, in Stockholm, Sweden.

More Quotes From Descartes

"Staying as I am, one foot in one country and the other in another, I find my condition very happy, in that it is free."

"With me, everything turns into mathematics."

If you are to be kept right, you must possess either good friends or red-hot enemies. The one will warn you, the other will expose you.

—Diogenes of Sinope

Diogenes of Sinope

Diogenes, born in 412 BCE in the Greek colony Sinope, was a Greek philosopher and one of the founders of Cynicism, which says the purpose of life is to live in agreement with nature and to reject possessions. He was a controversial figure in his time and was a very critical of culture. He toughened himself against nature, sleeping and eating where he wanted and often calling his home the inside of a tub. He settled in Athens, and became a student of Antisthenes, an ascetic and the father of Cynicism. Antisthenes originally refused to take students, but Diogenes followed him everywhere he went until Antisthenes relented.

Diogenes infused his philosophical teaching with a sense of humor that was unique among the philosophers of the time. He thought that people rely too heavily on preconceived notions of the nature of evil. He believed in rejecting societal mores; as an ascetic, he lived in a large ceramic urn outside of a temple. Once, when he saw a peasant boy drink from his hands, Diogenes broke his only bowl.

Diogenes was famous for challenging the elites of his day. He once embarrassed Plato who had defined a man as a "featherless biped." Diogenes presented a chicken at the Academy and declared, "Behold! I have brought you a man." Plato revised his definition, but publically thought Diogenes was mad.

Diogenes also is reported to have met Alexander the Great. He was said to have seen Diogenes studying a pile of human bones. Alexander asked him what he was doing, and Diogenes responded that he was looking for the bones of the King's father, but "could not distinguish them from those of a slave."

Diogenes died in Corinth in 323 BCE.

I prefer to be true to myself, even at the hazard of incurring the ridicule of others, rather than to be false, and incur my own abhorrence.

Frederick Douglass

Douglass, Frederick

After escaping from slavery, Frederick Douglass dedicated his life to fighting first for emancipation and later for women's suffrage. An orator, philosopher, and freedom fighter, he became the first African-American to hold high office in the U.S. government.

Frederick Douglass was born into slavery Maryland circa 1818. He lived with his maternal grandmother at first and later in the home of the plantation owner, who may have been his father. When he was twelve he was sent to Boston, where he learned to read and write. It was there that he began to read *The Columbian Orator*, a collection of political and philosophical essays, which shaped his views on freedom and human rights. At sixteen, Douglass was sent to work for Edward Covey, who had a reputation as a "slave-breaker." Covey whipped and beat Douglass mercilessly until one day, when he fought back, beating Covey, who never assaulted him again.

Escape and Abolitionism

In 1838, after two failed attempts, Douglass escaped to freedom with the help of Anna Murray, a free black woman from Baltimore. He made his way from Maryland to New York in less than a day. Murray met him there, and they married, settling in New Bedford, Massachusetts, a thriving community of free blacks. Douglass began to attend abolitionist meetings, and subscribed to *The Liberator*, William Lloyd Garrison's abolitionist newspaper. He began giving lectures on anti-slavery, and eventually spoke at the annual convention of the Massachusetts Anti-Slavery Society.

Garrison encouraged Douglass to write his autobiography; *Narrative of the Life of Frederick Douglass, an American Slave*, was published in 1845 and became a best seller. Following the publication, which made him a national figure, Douglass travelled to Europe to avoid recapture. He lived in Great Britain for two years, where he regularly spoke about the evils of slavery. After his supporters collected funds to buy his freedom, Douglass was able to return to the United States as a free man in 1847.

Women's Suffrage

Douglass began publishing several abolitionist newspapers of his own, the most famous of which is *The North Star*, whose motto was "Right is of no sex, truth is of no color, God is the Father of us all, and we are all brethren." In 1848 he attended the first convention on women's rights in Seneca Falls, where he spoke in favor of a resolution, proposed by Elizabeth Cady Stanton, which stated women's suffrage as a goal of the movement. Douglass said that the world would be improved if women were included in politics, and that he could not accept his right to vote as a black man if the right were not also extended to women. The resolution passed.

The Civil War and Reconstruction

During the Civil War, Douglass fought for the rights of black soldiers to join the Union Army, arguing that if the aim of the war was to end slavery, blacks must be allowed to fight. He also met with President Abraham Lincoln to discuss the treatment of black soldiers in the Union Army. In 1863, upon the Emancipation Proclamation, he criticized the fact that it only freed slaves in Confederate states. He also was publically disappointed that Lincoln did not support suffrage for black freedmen, and supported his opponent in the 1864 election.

Following the war, Douglass was appointed to a number of government positions, including diplomat to the Dominican Republic and president of the Freedmen's Savings Bank during Reconstruction. He praised President Ulysses Grant's signing of the 1871 Civil Rights Act, which was designed to combat the Ku Klux Klan and other white terror organizations in the South. In 1889 he was appointed consul-general to Haiti.

Frederick Douglass continued fighting for the rights of women and blacks until his death. On February 20, 1895, after attending a meeting of the National Council of Women, he died at his home. He is buried in Rochester, New York.

More Quotes From Frederick Douglass

"They cannot degrade Frederick Douglass. The soul that is within me no man can degrade. I am not the one that is being degraded on account of this treatment, but those who are inflicting it upon me ..."

"The man who is right is a majority. We, who have God and conscience on our side, have a majority against the universe."

"You have seen how a man was made a slave; you shall see how a slave was made a man."

"I appear this evening as a thief and a robber. I stole this head, these limbs, this body from my master, and ran off with them."

"I make no pretension to patriotism. So long as my voice can be heard on this or the other side of the Atlantic, I will hold up America to the lightning scorn of moral indignation. In doing this, I shall feel myself discharging the duty of a true patriot; for he is a lover of his country who rebukes and does not excuse its sins. It is righteousness that exalteth a nation while sin is a reproach to any people."

> *The cost of liberty is less than the price of repression.*
>
> *W.E.B. Du Bois*

Du Bois, W.E.B.

W.E.B. Du Bois was a historian, author, activist, and one of the leaders of the struggle to obtain civil rights for African-Americans during the first half of the twentieth century. He co-founded the National Association for the Advancement of Colored People.

William Edward Burghardt Du Bois was born in Great Barrington, Massachusetts, on February 23, 1868, in Great Barrington, Massachusetts. He was able to attend school with white classmates, and his white teachers supported his academic studies. In 1885 he was accepted to Fisk University, a historically black college in Nashville, Tennessee. It was while he was in Nashville that Du Bois had his first encounters with Jim Crow laws and found himself treated as a second-class citizen. While he was at Fisk, he began developing a deep awareness of the viciousness of American racism.

After graduating from Fisk with a bachelor's degree, he attended Harvard College from 1888–1890, where he graduated cum laude with a bachelor's in history. He supported himself with scholarships and summer jobs while he studied. He began a graduate program in sociology at Harvard in 1891, and traveled to the University of Berlin to study at Humboldt-Universität. While he was in Germany, Du Bois was exposed to progressive political views and studied with some of the most prominent sociologists of the time. In 1895 he became the first African-American to receive a Ph.D. from Harvard.

Writing and Activism

In 1894 Du Bois accepted a teaching position at Wilberforce University in Ohio. While there, he married Nina Gomer in 1896. That summer, he accepted a year-long research appointment at the University of Pennsylvania. While there he conducted sociological field work in the poor African-American neighborhoods of Philadelphia. In 1899 Du Bois published his findings in the first sociological case study of the African-American community, titled *The Philadelphia Negro: A Social Study*. His study found that racial segregation was a highly negative factor in social outcomes in African-American communities. In *The Philadelphia Negro,* Du Bois coined the term "the talented tenth," which he used to describe the probability of one in ten African-American men becoming leaders of their community.

Du Bois published *Strivings of the Negro People* in 1897, an article that argued against Frederick Douglass' assertion that

African-Americans should integrate into white society. Instead, he wrote, African-Americans should embrace their roots while striving to secure a place in American society. That same year, he accepted a position at Atlanta University. While there, he produced dozens of academic papers and began hosting the annual Atlanta Conference of Negro Problems. He gained national prominence when he spoke out against Booker T. Washington's Atlanta Compromise. The Atlanta Compromise proposed that African-Americans in the South should submit to white rule, provided they were guaranteed education and economic opportunities. Dubois argued that African-Americans were guaranteed equal rights by the Fourteenth Amendment, and should fight for them.

In 1903 Du Bois wrote *The Souls of Black Folk*, a collection of essays on race. In it, he argues that African-Americans in the South deserve the right to vote, education, and equal treatment before the law. He also discusses his opposition to the Atlanta Compromise, and the Black experience in America. Although Du Bois was not the first to use the term "color line" to refer to segregation (it dates back to at least 1881, when it was used by Frederick Douglass), the essays in this book did emphasize the term and bring it to prominence.

Du Bois co-founded the National Association for the Advancement of Colored People in 1909, and edited *The Crisis*, its monthly publication. The NAACP challenged Jim Crow laws with test cases in the courts, and organized political opposition to segregation in marches. By 1920 the organization had nearly 90,000 members.

W.E.B. Du Bois died on August 27, 1963, in Accra, Ghana. The next day, Dr. Martin Luther King Jr. delivered the iconic "I Have a Dream" speech at the March on Washington.

More Quotes From W.E.B. Du Bois

"Liberty trains for liberty. Responsibility is the first step in responsibility."

"The cause of war is preparation for war."

"The problem of the twentieth century is the problem of the color line."

"There is but one coward on earth, and that is the coward that dare not know."

"To be a poor man is hard, but to be a poor race in a land of dollars is the very bottom of hardships."

"The worker must work for the glory of his handiwork, not simply for pay; the thinker must think for truth, not for fame."

"The function of the university is not simply to teach bread-winning, or to furnish teachers for the public schools or to be a centre of polite society; it is, above all, to be the organ of that fine adjustment between real life and the growing knowledge of life, an adjustment which forms the secret of civilization."

> # *Pleasure is the beginning and end of living happily.*
> —Epicurus

Epicurus

Epicurus, the Greek philosopher, wanted his students to live without fear or pain. He found that the meaning of life was not to be looked for in the invisible realms of spirit and rationale, but in the material world that surrounds us.

Epicurus was born on the small Greek island of Samos in 341 BCE. His father was a schoolteacher, and the family was poor. He began developing his own ideas at a young age, having growing disillusioned with his teachers. After a number of years travelling around ancient Greece, in about 306 BCE Epicurus established a school in Athens called The Garden, where he lived and taught for the remainder of his life. Here he developed and spread his philosophy of Epicureanism: the pursuit of pleasure.

His philosophy, which taught that the goal of life is pleasure, has since given rise to the use of the word *epicurean* to mean "gourmet," but this is at odds with his original meaning. Epicurus considered pleasure to be attainable by living in contemplative moderation. He taught his students to shed anxieties and desires and enjoy the natural happiness that is found in the freedom from fear and absence of pain, called *ataraxia* and *aponia*, respectively.

Epicurus believed there are no gods that can harm humans, and likewise there is no afterlife. He taught that the things we actually need are easy to find, and those that make us suffer are easy to endure. According to him, one could only live a "pleasant" life by also living "wisely, well, and justly." Epicurus promoted egalitarianism at his school, accepting women and slaves, which was highly unusual at the time. His teachings have since influenced many great thinkers: among others, John Locke and Thomas Jefferson included his ideas about the pursuit of happiness in their own works.

More Quotes From Epicurus

"Don't fear god, / Don't worry about death; / What is good is easy to get, and / What is terrible is easy to endure."

"He who is not satisfied with a little, is satisfied with nothing."

"Self-sufficiency is the greatest of all wealth."

"Let no one be slow to seek wisdom when he is young nor weary in the search of it when he has grown old. For no age is too early or too late for the health of the soul."

Leave no stone unturned.

—Euripides

Euripides

Along with Sophocles and Aechylus, Euripides was one of the three tragedians of ancient Greece whose works have survived. Euripides wrote more than ninety plays in his lifetime, nineteen of which have survived.

Euripides was born in Salamis in 480 BCE. When he was a young boy, his father received an oracle that said Euripides would "win crowns of victory." His father assumed that meant he would be a great athlete, and sent him to train as one, but he also studied philosophy and the arts. He won his first crown of victory in 441 BCE in the annual Athenian festival of the arts, and would go on to win four more during his life.

Some of Euripides' most famous tragedies are *Medea, The Bacchae, Hippolytus*, and *Alcestis*. He pioneered the portrayal of heroes and gods as ordinary figures who were faced with extraordinary circumstances, which would influence later comic and romantic plays. Euripides also invented the style of focusing on the inner lives of his characters and exploring the workings of human psychology, which was entirely new to Greek theatre.

Euripides was distinctive among the ancient Athenian writers in the sympathy he extended to all of his characters, including women, which was unusual at the time. This practice often shocked his conservative audiences. Because of this, he was often compared to Socrates as one of the leaders of a corrupting movement of intellectual decadence. In 408 BCE he chose to voluntarily exile himself in Macedonia. He would live there until his death in 406 BCE.

More Quotes From Euripides

"Those whom God wishes to destroy, he first makes mad."

"A sweet thing, for whatever time, to revisit in dreams the dear dead we have lost."

"God, these old men! How they pray for death."

"Today's today. Tomorrow we may be ourselves gone down the drain of Eternity."

"There is no benefit in the gifts of a bad man."

"We know the good, we apprehend it clearly, but we can't bring it to achievement."

You can't build a reputation on what you are going to do.

Henry Ford

Ford, Henry

Henry Ford's innovative use of the assembly line to manufacture the Model T Ford made automobiles widely affordable for the first time, significantly impacting the industry and landscape of twentieth century America.

Henry Ford was born on his parents' farm near Dearborn, Michigan, on July 30, 1863. He was a very inquisitive child, and always trying to figure out how things worked. On his thirteenth birthday his father gave him a pocket watch. Ford immediately took the watch apart and put it back together. His father's friends and neighbors soon heard about his abilities, and they were soon asking young Henry to fix their watches when they stopped working. When he was sixteen years old, feeling unfulfilled by farm work, he left home and went to Detroit, where he got a job working as a machinist's apprentice at a shipyard. While there, he learned how to build and repair steam engines along with bookkeeping.

In 1888 he married Clara Bryant, and for a few years he went back to farming to support his young family. In 1891 he secured a job as an engineer at the Edison Illuminating Company, and within two years he was promoted to a chief engineer at the company. His promotion allowed him enough money to begin experimenting with gasoline-powered horseless carriages. He successfully constructed his first model, the Ford Quadricycle, in 1896. In a meeting with company executives, he presented his plans to Thomas Edison, who encouraged him to keep working on his design.

The Ford Motor Company

Ford continued improving his horseless carriage, and in 1903 he founded the Ford Motor Company with his old friend Alexander Malcomson and a group of investors that included the Dodge brothers. On October 1, 1908, the company introduced the Model T, which had a simple design that made it both easy to repair and inexpensive to buy. The car was soon everywhere. Sales were steadily increasing, and for the next several years, the Ford Motor Company posted profit gains of 100%. In his autobiography, he writes of this time:

"Therefore in 1909 I announced one morning, without any previous warning, that in the future we were going to build only one model, that the model was going to be 'Model T,' and that the chassis would be exactly the same for all cars, and I remarked: 'Any customer can have a car painted any colour that he wants so long as it is black.' I cannot say that any one agreed with me."

In 1913, in order to increase efficiency in manufacturing the Model T, he introduced the moving assembly line to his factories. The system was conceived of by a group of production executives at the company, and it made it possible to produce Model Ts at an astonishing rate. It also allowed the company to reduce the price of the car, making it widely accessible. Ford introduced a wage of five dollars a day in 1914 along with profit sharing for long-term employees, which attracted highly skilled mechanics to his assembly lines and ensured low worker turnover. In 1926 he reduced the company's work week from six days to five.

Political Beliefs

Ford was strongly opposed to unions, believing they curtailed worker productivity. He also, for several years, employed a "Social Department" that intruded on his employee's private lives, investigating their behavior away from work before they could be approved for profit sharing. These were not the only areas in which his views were controversial; Ford was also a vehement anti-Semite. He went so far as to publish an anti-Semitic newspaper called *The Dearborn Independent* and a four-volume collection of anti-Semitic conspiracy theories called *The International Jew*. He was praised by Heinrich Himmler and Adolf Hitler, who based his production of the Volkswagen on Ford's Model T.

Henry Ford died on April 7, 1947, near his home in Dearborn, Michigan.

More Quotes From Henry Ford

"An idealist is a person who helps other people to be prosperous."

"Any customer can have a car painted any color that he wants so long as it is black."

"Thinking is the hardest work there is, which is probably the reason why so few engage in it."

Love your Enemies, for they tell you your Faults.

Franklin, Benjamin

Inventor, writer, postmaster, statesman, diplomat, and Founding Father, Benjamin Franklin helped write the Declaration of Independence, made important discoveries in the sciences, and left an enduring legacy. He is often called "The First American" for his contributions to the nation.

Benjamin Franklin was born in Boston on January 17, 1706. He attended the Boston Latin School until he was ten, when he began working for his father, a candlemaker. When he was twelve, his older brother Josiah apprenticed him at his printing shop. He left Boston in 1723 and settled in Philadelphia, where he found work in another printing shop. He traveled to London in 1724, returning to Philadelphia in 1726; the same year he developed his "Thirteen Virtues," which he attempted to practice for the rest of his life. He opened his own printing shop in Philadelphia in 1728. In 1730 he became common-law husband to Deborah Read, with whom he had had an on-again, off-again relationship for several years. Franklin founded a study and debate group called the Junto, and when its members ran out of books to read, Franklin helped found the first public library in America in 1731.

Publications and Experiments

Franklin began publishing *Poor Richard's Almanack* in 1732, and it quickly became very popular. The almanac provided weather forecasts, poetry, and essays, and it was where many of Franklin's popular aphorisms first appeared. Franklin would publish the almanac for a quarter century. He spent the next two decades growing his businesses; by 1748 he was one of the wealthiest men in Philadelphia. He left his partner in charge of his printing business and began spending more time in scientific pursuits, and founded the American Philosophical Society. That same year he bought his first slaves. Franklin's views on slavery would eventually change, and he freed them in the 1760s.

In 1751 Franklin published *Experiments and Observations on Electricity*, which compiled several years' worth of his investigations. The following year he proved that lightning was electricity with his famous key and kite experiment, and invented the lightning rod. Among his other inventions were bifocals, the rocking chair, the flexible catheter, and a public firefighting brigade.

American Revolution

In 1765 the British Parliament passed the Stamp Act, which imposed a tax on all printed material used in the colonies. Franklin, serving as Pennsylvania's agent in London, delivered a passionate speech denouncing the Act in Parliament that contributed to its repeal the following year. In 1768, he wrote the pamphlet *Causes of the American Discontents Before 1768*, and in 1775 he returned to Philadelphia to assist in the cause of independence. He was elected to the Second Continental

Congress that year, and in 1776 he helped write the Declaration of Independence. He was then sent to France to negotiate for the French King's financial and military support. He remained there for nine years, and became the informal American ambassador to Louis XVI's court. In 1783 he was instrumental in negotiating the Treaty of Paris, which ended the war and granted the colonies their independence.

Franklin returned to Philadelphia in 1785 and represented Pennsylvania at the Constitutional Convention of 1787. He played an integral role in developing the Great Compromise, which resulted in proportional representation for the States in the House of Representatives and equal representation in the Senate. The compromise was vital for ensuring the ratification of the Constitution.

Benjamin Franklin died in Philadelphia on April 17, 1790.

More Quotes From Benjamin Franklin

"If all printers were determined not to print anything till they were sure it would offend nobody, there would be very little printed."

"Ambition has its disappointments to sour us, but never the good fortune to satisfy us."

"Sell not virtue to purchase wealth, nor Liberty to purchase power."

"[A] great Empire, like a great Cake, is most easily diminished at the Edges."

> *Being entirely honest with oneself is a good exercise.*

Sigm. Freud

Freud, Sigmund

As it turns out, the "Father of Psychoanalysis" didn't do much self-evaluation and was a case study of neurotic behavior.

A neurologist and psychiatrist, Sigmund Freud's research on human behavior left a lasting impact on the field of psychology.

Freud himself was not without issues. He was a heavy smoker—smoking as many as twenty cigars a day for most of his life—and as a result, endured more than thirty operations for mouth cancer. In the 1880s he conducted extensive research on cocaine, advocating use of the drug as a cure for a number of ills, including depression. Reports indicate that Freud was probably addicted to cocaine for several years during this time period. And a friend for whom he prescribed cocaine was later diagnosed with "cocaine psychosis" and subsequently died in what is referred to by biographers as the "cocaine incident."

Freud suffered psychosomatic disorders and phobias, including agoraphobia (a fear of crowded spaces) and a fear of dying. Though his *Theory of Sexuality* was being widely denounced as a threat to morality, he decided that sexual activity was incompatible with accomplishing great work and stopped having sexual relations with his wife. Yet he is thought to have had a long affair with his wife's sister, Minna Bernays, who lived with the couple. Freud denied these persistent rumors, but in 2006, a German researcher uncovered a century-old guest book at a Swiss hotel in which Freud registered himself and Minna as "Dr. Freud and wife."

Freud fled his native Austria after the Nazi Anschluss in 1938 and spent his last year of life in London. Dying from mouth cancer, in September 1939, he convinced his doctor to help him commit suicide with injections of morphine.

More Quotes From Sigmund Freud

"How bold one gets when one is sure of being loved."

"The interpretation of dreams is the royal road to a knowledge of the unconscious activities of the mind."

"Psychoanalysis is in essence a cure through love."

> *Genius will not live and thrive without training, but it does not the less reward the watering pot and pruning knife.*
>
> —Margaret Fuller

Fuller, Margaret

A feminist, transcendentalist, journalist, and revolutionary Margaret Fuller wrote the first feminist book in the United States.

Margaret Fuller was born in Cambridge, Massachusetts, on May 23, 1810. Her father, a lawyer and politician, began educating her at a young age, and Fuller was literate by the age of four. He did not allow him to read the kind of novellas and books on etiquette that were typically given to girls of the day, instead teaching her Latin and giving her the classics to read. Her father was rather overbearing, and his insistence on precision in Fuller's lessons gave her nightmares and caused her to sleepwalk.

Fuller attended school beginning in 1821, and when she was fourteen she was sent to Boston to attend a boarding school for young women. Upon finishing she returned to her family home in Cambridge, where she continued studying classical philosophy, several languages, and literature. In 1833 her family moved to rural Groton, Massachusetts, where Fuller was isolated and had to manage the household when her mother fell ill. She published her first piece of literary criticism in the *Western Messenger* in 1835. Her father died in October of that year, which devastated Fuller.

Transcendentalism and Writing

Fuller visited Ralph Waldo Emerson in 1836 and secured a job that year teaching in Boston, and later in Providence, Rhode Island. In 1839 she returned to Boston and began hosting discussion groups with prominent women from New England. These "Conversations" would continue until 1844, and Fuller intended them to supplant the education so many women were denied at the time, and covered natural philosophy, history, literature and the arts.

In 1839 Fuller also co-founded a transcendentalist journal, *The Dial*, with Ralph Waldo Emerson. She began editing the journal in 1840, and quickly became widely recognized as one of the leaders of the movement. She regularly visited Brook Farm, a transcendentalist

community nine miles outside of Boston. In 1844 she travelled through the Midwest, and wrote *Summer on the Lake* about her journey. The book met some acclaim, and Horace Greeley, the editor of the *New York Tribune*, invited her to join the newspaper as a literary critic.

Woman in the Nineteenth Century

In 1845 Fuller wrote one of her best-known works, *Woman in the Nineteenth Century*. The book was the first major feminist work published in the United States. It originally appeared in serial format in *The Dial* as "The Great Lawsuit: Man vs. Men, Woman vs. Women." In it, she argued that the European heritage of the United States has prevented America from ever reaching true equality, and that its treatment of Native Americans and African Americans was a result of this inherited immorality. She argues for the practice of divine love to right these wrongs. Fuller says that only be elevating women to be the equals of men can this kind of divine love be truly achieved. She defines four kinds of marriage, which she ranks from least to best: the shared household, mutual idolatry, intellectual companionship, and religious union. These ideas blend transcendentalist philosophy with feminism in a landmark work.

In 1846 the *Tribune* sent Fuller to Europe as a correspondent. She travelled to Italy, where she met Giovanni Angelo. In 1848 they had a son together, and the next year they took part in a rebellion that attempted to establish a Roman Republic. The rebellion failed, and they fled to Florence before boarding a ship to New York. The ship ran aground during a storm on July 19, 1850. Their bodies were never recovered.

More Quotes From Margaret Fuller

"It is astonishing what force, purity, and wisdom it requires for a human being to keep clear of falsehoods."

"Beware of over-great pleasure in being popular or even beloved."

"Might the simple maxim, that honesty is the best policy be laid to heart! Might a sense of the true aims of life elevate the tone of politics and trade, till public and private honor become identical!"

"Very early, I knew that the only object in life was to grow."

"Your prudence, my wise friend, allows too little room for the mysterious whisperings of life."

"All around us lies what we neither understand nor use. Our capacities, our instincts for this our present sphere are but half developed."

"There exists in the minds of men a tone of feeling toward women as toward slaves."

> *Victory attained by violence is tantamount to a defeat, for it is momentary.*

mkGandhi

Gandhi, Mohandas

Mahatma Gandhi was the leader of India's independence movement, and pioneered the use of nonviolent civil disobedience to challenge powerful governments. His philosophy would influence many important movements in the twentieth century, including the American Civil Rights Movement.

Mohandas Karamchand Gandhi was born in Kathiawar, India, on October 2, 1869. At age thirteen he was married to Kasturba Makanji, and was a shy teenager. His family encouraged him to enter the legal profession, and in 1888 he travelled to London to study the law. When he returned to India in 1891, he initially struggled in his legal practice, and in 1893 he obtained a one year contract to work as a lawyer in South Africa. Upon arriving there, he was disgusted by the extreme racial segregation he witnessed.

Political Awakening

On June 7, 1893, while he was travelling by train, a white South African objected to him riding in the first-class railcar, and demanded he move to the rear of the train. Gandhi refused, and was thrown off the train at the next station. The next year, he founded the Natal Indian Congress to fight segregation. At the end of his contract, he remained in South Africa to organize against racial injustice. His legal practice expanded while he was there. During World War I he organized an all-Indian ambulance corps for the British, believing that it would advance the cause of Indian self-determination. While in South Africa he began studying world religions.

In 1906 Gandhi organized his first *Satyagraha*, or "truth and firmness," a campaign of civil disobedience to protest the South African government's treatment of Indians. Hundreds of protestors, including Gandhi, were imprisoned. In 1913 Gandhi negotiated concessions from the government, including recognition of Hindu marriages. He returned to India in 1915.

Fight for Independence

Upon his return, Gandhi founded an ashram, or hermitage, that was receptive to all castes, which was unusual at the time. He lived as an ascetic, devoting himself to prayer, meditation, and fasting, and wore only a simple shawl and loincloth. In 1919 the Rowlatt Act was passed, which permitted authorities to imprison

Indians without trial. Gandhi organized a Satyagraha campaign of peaceful demonstrations. On April 13 British troops opened fire on a peaceful crowd, slaughtering nearly a thousand people. Gandhi assumed leadership of the Indian National Congress and called for a general strike. He was arrested in 1922 and pled guilty to sedition. He was released in 1924.

The Salt Satyagraha

In 1930 Gandhi organized a Satyagraha to protest the British monopoly on salt in India. He led a few dozen followers on a 240-mile march across Indian to the Arabian Sea. There, he made salt from evaporated seawater in a symbolic act of defiance. The Salt Satyagraha sparked a wave of civil disobedience across India, and more than sixty-thousand people were imprisoned for similar acts. The 1930 protests elevated Gandhi to a worldwide figure, and he was named *Time Magazine's* Man of the Year while he was still being held in prison for his act.

Independence

In 1931 Gandhi was released from prison, and negotiated to end the Salt Satyagraha in exchange for the release of thousands of political prisoners. He attended the London Round Table Conference to attempt to press for home rule, but was unable to secure concessions from the British. He returned to India, and was imprisoned again in 1932 by Viceroy Willingdon. He was eventually released, and left the Indian National Congress in 1934.

After Britain's influence was diminished following World War II, the Indian National Congress and the Muslim League jointly negotiated with Parliament for independence. Gandhi promoted a united India, but the final plan partitioned the subcontinent into two states: Muslim Pakistan and Hindu India. A wave of terrible violence swept the subcontinent, with attacks and reprisals between Muslims and Hindus leaving hundreds dead. Gandhi appealed for peace and expressed sympathy for Muslims, which enraged many Hindus who came to view him as a traitor.

On January 30, 1948, Nathuram Godse, a Hindu extremist who was angry at Gandhi's promotion of tolerance toward Muslims, shot him while he was on his way to a prayer meeting, killing him.

More Quotes From Mohandas Gandhi

"In reality there are as many religions as there are individuals."

"The weak can never forgive. Forgiveness is the attribute of the strong."

"It is not possible to make a person or society non-violent by compulsion."

"Any action that is dictated by fear or by coercion of any kind ceases to be moral."

"In matters of conscience, the law of majority has no place."

"No action which is not voluntary can be called moral."

> *Instruction does much, but encouragement everything.*

Goethe, Johann Wolfgang von

An incredibly prolific writer, Goethe produced what is considered the greatest masterpiece in the history of German literature.

Johann Wolfgang von Goethe was born in Frankfurt, Germany, on August 28, 1749. His family was upper-middle class. Goethe's father, a lawyer, educated him until he was sixteen, until Goethe went to Leipzig to study the law as well. While he was at law school he began writing poetry and plays. Because of a long illness, his studies were put on hold; he finished law school in 1771. In 1772 Goethe wrote his first major play, *Gotz von Berlichingen*. Two years later he completed the novel *The Sorrows of Young*

Werther. Both were well-received and established Goethe's reputation as a writer and the leader of the "Romantic Revolt," a literary movement that was occurring in Germany.

The Duke of Weimar invited Goethe to join his court in 1775, and he served there as the director of the Ministries of Finance, Agriculture, and Mines for the next ten years. The two became good friends, and the Duke invited numerous other artists and writers to his court. Goethe, however, found that his administrative duties were interfering with his literary endeavors, and he left the court in 1786, travelling to Italy to pursue his art. When he returned to Germany, the Duke appointed him the director of the Weimar State Theatre and granted him a generous stipend that allowed Goethe to focus on writing.

Faust

Goethe married his mistress, with whom he'd had a son seventeen years earlier in 1806. His literary success brought him fame throughout Germany and Europe, and Napoleon was among his admirers. Goethe produced more than 140 volumes of work in his lifetime, but his most famous work is perhaps *Faust*. The tragic play was completed in two parts; the first was finished in 1808 and the second in 1832. The play is generally considered the greatest work of German literature. It is a retelling of a classic German legend: Faust, a successful and talented scholar, is God's favorite human being, and is attempting to learn all there is that can be known. Mephistopheles, a demon, makes a wager with God that he can turn Faust away from God. God accepts the bet, and Mephistopheles pays Faust a visit.

Faust's studies have stalled, and the demon makes him an offer: he will do anything Faust wants while he is alive, but when he dies he must serve Mephistopheles in hell. Faust agrees. The demon helps him seduce a woman named Gretchen, but when Gretchen accidentally kills her mother, her brother challenges Faust, who, with the demon's help, kills him. Gretchen, who has had a child with Faust, drowns the baby and is imprisoned for murder. Faust attempts to free her, but she refuses to go with him, and he flees. In part two, Faust awakens in a field, having forgotten the events of part one. He has a series of adventures in which Mephistopheles helps him become a powerful figure. When he dies, Mephistopheles attempts to claim his soul, but he is rescued by angels, who carry him to heaven.

In addition to his numerous works for the stage, Goethe wrote many novels, including *Egemont* in 1788, *Pandora* in 1810, and *Wilhelm Meister's Journeys* in 1829. He also published short stories, collections of poetry, and even scientific treatises such as *The Theory of Colors*, written in 1810. Goethe died on March 22, 1832, already considered one of the greatest writers in German history.

More Quotes From Johann Wolfgang von Goethe

"There is strong shadow where there is much light."

"He alone is great and happy who fills his own station of independence, and has neither to command nor to obey."

"One lives but once in the world."

"When young, one is confident to be able to build palaces for mankind, but when the time comes one has one's hands full just to be able to remove their trash."

"A noble person attracts noble people, and knows how to hold on to them."

"Investigate what is, and not what pleases."

"Patriotism ruins history."

"One must be something in order to do something."

"If I work incessantly to the last, nature owes me another form of existence when the present one collapses."

No lasting gain has ever come from compulsion.

—Samuel Gompers

Gompers, Samuel

Samuel Gompers was one of the most significant leaders of the early labor movement. He cofounded and was the first president of the American Federation of Labor.

Samuel Gompers was born in London on January 27, 1850, to a very poor family. He attended a free Jewish school when he was six years old, where he learned to read and write. When he was thirteen, his family immigrated to the United States, settling in New York City. Gompers began working with his father as a cigar-maker. They joined the Cigar-Makers' Union, and Gompers quickly rose to a leadership position in the organization. He built the Union into a successful organization despite the advent of technological advances that could threaten cigar-makers' jobs.

In 1881 Gompers helped organize an informal association of several unions in order to promote collective bargaining across trades. The loose affiliation was formally organized into the American Federation of Labor (AFL) in 1886. Gompers became its president, and was the first leader of a national union who encouraged using strikes as an effective weapon to put pressure on employers. He was vehemently opposed to the Socialist faction within the AFL, believing that they acted toward political ends rather than toward securing conditions from employers. An immigrant himself, he opposed open immigration from Europe for fear that it would lower wages in the United States. He supported the U.S. invasion of Cuba during the Spanish Civil War, believing that it would improve conditions of cigar-makers there.

After a long illness, Gompers died on December 13, 1924, in San Antonio, Texas.

More Quotes From Samuel Gompers

"[The labor movement is] a movement of the working people, for the working people, by the working people, governed by ourselves, with its policies determined by ourselves ... "

"The trade union movement represents the organized economic power of the workers ... It is in reality the most potent and the most direct social insurance the workers can establish."

"What does labor want? We want more schoolhouses and less jails; more books and less arsenals; more learning and less vice; more leisure and less greed; more justice and less revenge; in fact, more of the opportunities to cultivate our better natures."

> # Go West, young man.
> *Horace Greeley*

Greeley, Horace

Although we know Horace Greeley wrote the phrase, and was certainly the most prominent person to say it in a memorable way, do we know for sure that it was Greeley who actually coined this pioneering piece of advice?

Horace Greeley was a self-made newspaperman, social critic, and advocate who built the influential *New York Tribune* into a mighty voice for change. He opposed monopolies, the death penalty, and slavery, and he advocated homestead land grants and egalitarianism. In a *Tribune* editorial dated July 13, 1865, Greeley wrote, "Washington is not a place to live in. The rents are high, the food is bad, the dust is disgusting and the morals are deplorable. Go West, young man, go West and grow up with the country."

Although he was a solid advocate for Western settlement, Greeley was attempting to speak to a different issue. He was addressing disgruntled civil servants in D.C. who had complained at length about low pay and high living costs in their city of employment. What Greeley meant was, "If you don't like it here, go somewhere else."

A number of historians credit the phrase to John B. Soule, writing in the *Terre Haute Express* in 1851. That credit lacks one key component: a specific date. If we're sure someone said or wrote something, we usually know exactly when. With Soule, we do not, so a firm credit becomes problematic. He probably did say it, but just as likely, so did others before and after. In the 1800s many thousands sought their fortunes out West. "Go West" was the era's equivalent of saying, "Apply to college."

Greeley's own story ended less optimistically. He ran against Ulysses S. Grant for president, was soundly defeated, lost his mind and his newspaper, and died insane. His assessment of Washington, D.C., however, has in many ways endured the test of time.

More Quotes From Horace Greeley

"The masses of our countrymen, North and South, are eager to clasp hands across the bloody chasm which has so long divided them."

"The illusion that times that were are better than those that are, has probably pervaded all ages."

"No man, for any considerable period, can wear one face to himself, and another to the multitude, without finally getting bewildered as to which may be true."

Nath' Hawthorne

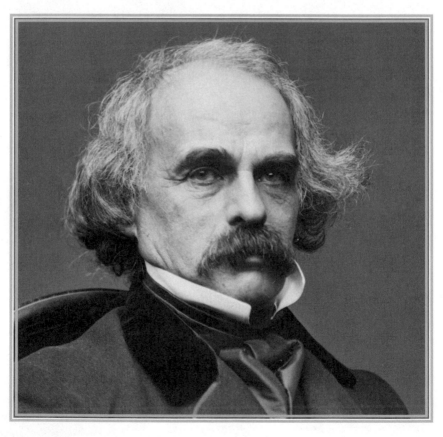

Hawthorne, Nathaniel

His novel *The Scarlet Letter* is one of the great works of classic American literature.

Nathaniel Hawthorne was born on the Fourth of July, 1804, in Salem, Massachusetts. Hawthorne's family was descended from some of the earliest Puritan settlers of Salem; more than 150 years before his birth, his ancestor John Hathorne was one of the judges who presided over the Salem Witch Trials in the seventeenth century. When he learned this, the author changed his name to "Hawthorne" in order to distance himself from his ancestors. Hawthorne's father died at sea when Nathaniel was only four years old. When he broke his leg as a boy, he was bedridden for several months, and during this time he developed a love of reading and decided he would become a writer. Hawthorne studied at Bowdoin College from 1821–1825, where he became friends with Henry Wadsworth Longfellow and other writers.

After graduation Hawthorne returned to Salem, where he began writing. He published *Fanshawe*, his first novel, in 1828, to positive reviews. He began publishing short stories in literary journals, and these were collected in *Twice-Told Tales* in 1837. In 1838 he was engaged to Sophia Peabody, a transcendentalist, and they married in 1842. The two stayed briefly at the Brook Farm, a transcendentalist commune, where he met Ralph Waldo Emerson and Henry David Thoreau. Hawthorne's early writing did not provide for a steady income, and so he worked at the Boston Custom House weighing salt and coal.

The Scarlet Letter

In 1846 Hawthorne was hired as a surveyor at the Salem Custom House, which gave his family some financial security, but also interfered with his writing. Following the election of Zachary Taylor, Hawthorne, a Democrat, lost this politically-connected appointment. He initially protested his dismissal in a letter to the *Boston Daily Advertiser*, but soon found that his dismissal allowed him the free time to work on his writing again. His next novel, *The Scarlet Letter*, published in 1850, would catapult him to fame, be one of the first mass produced books in the United States, and become a classic of American literature.

The novel draws on Hawthorne's own Puritan roots, and is set in Puritan Boston in the seventeenth century. It opens with the protagonist, Hester Prynne, being punished for the crime of adultery. She is made to stand on a platform in the town square, and must wear a scarlet *A* on her dress. Her husband, who was thought to have been lost at sea, is at the edge of the crowd, and he swears to find the father of Hester's illegitimate child. Hester refuses to reveal the name of the father to the authorities or to her husband, and goes to raise her daughter, Pearl, on the outskirts of town. Years later, her husband discovers that the Reverend Dimmesdale is Pearl's father. Dimmesdale suffers psychologically from his guilt. Eventually Dimmesdale admits his guilt to the town and dies in Hester's arms. Hester is later buried near his grave, and they share a single tombstone with a scarlet letter *A* on it.

The novel's themes of guilt, repentance, and dignity in the face of repression made it one of the most influential American works of the nineteenth century. Hawthorne would write several more novels in his lifetime, as well as multiple collections of short stories. He was held in very high esteem by many of his peers, including Edgar Allan Poe, who called him "an indisputable genius."

Hawthorne died in his sleep on May 19, 1864, at Plymouth, New Hampshire.

More Quotes From Nathaniel Hawthorne

"If his inmost heart could have been laid open, there would have been discovered that dream of undying fame, which, dream as it is, is more powerful than a thousand realities."

"The young have less charity for aged follies than the old for those of youth."

"I have not lived, but only dreamed about living."

"How slowly I have made my way in life! How much is still to be done!"

"Nobody has any conscience about adding to the improbabilities of a marvelous tale."

"Every individual has a place to fill in the world, and is important, in some respect, whether he chooses to be so or not."

> ## *To be aware of limitations is already to be beyond them.*

∂ Hegel

Hegel, Georg Wilhelm Friedrich

Hegel's dialectics would become one of the most influential ideas in Western philosophy for the next hundred years.

Georg Wilhelm Friedrich Hegel was born in Stuttgart, Germany, on August 27, 1770. His father Georg was a civil servant, and his mother Maria was the daughter of a member of the Württemberg court. Maria taught him Latin as a child, and instilled in Hegel a lifelong love of learning. He attended an elite preparatory school before attending the Seminary at the University of Tübinge at his father's urging. While he was there he became interested in philosophy, and instead of joining the clergy, as his father had wanted, he became a private tutor and continued to study philosophy in his spare time.

Dialectics

Hegel's father died in 1799, leaving him with a modest inheritance that allowed him to spend more time working on developing his ideas about philosophy. Hegel's theories were based on the transcendental idealism of Immanuel Kant and the progressive political ideology of Rousseau, but ultimately reject Kant as overly restraining. He developed a new philosophy that attempted to create a systematic means of understanding world history. Hegel's ideas would become the philosophy that is known as *dialectics*, or the juxtaposition of two opposing arguments.

In 1801 Hegel published his first book, an examination of the relationship between religion and philosophy in which he rejected mysticism and argued for a rational basis of attempting to understand the self. He began giving lectures on logic and metaphysics, and in 1802 he began publishing a journal on philosophy with his friend and colleague Friedrich Schelling. Hegel's position as a lecturer was unpaid, and in 1806 he found his financial situation increasingly perilous. Under pressure to publish, he worked that year on what would become his magnum opus, *The Phenomenology of Spirit*, which was published in 1807. In it, he lays out his three-part philosophy of dialectics.

Dialectics was not new at the time—the notion had existed at least since Aristotle—but Hegel brought a modern understanding to the concept and applied it as a method for dissecting nature and history. Hegel's dialectics consist of three developmental parts: the thesis, or original state of things, which gives rise to the antithesis, or the reaction and contradiction to the thesis, and the synthesis, in which the thesis and antithesis are resolved. Hegel himself did not use these terms, preferring the abstract, negative, and concrete to describe the relationship, but the thesis/antithesis remains what he is popularly known for.

One of the major aspects that set Hegel's dialectics apart from the classical understanding of the idea was that it was not a concrete set of principles that describe the world as it is a methodology for attempting to understand it. Experiences, to Hegel, are valuable empirical data for observing the unfolding of the natural world and human history. He believed that the "totality" of experience is the sum of a series of experiences rather than something couched in an "absolute mind."

Hegel continued teaching, first at a school in Nuremberg from 1808–1815, and then as the chair of the philosophy department at the University of Berlin from 1816–1829. During this time he wrote the *Encyclopedia of the Philosophical Sciences, Elements of the Philosophy of Right*, and the *Philosophy of Spirit*.

Hegel died on November 14, 1831, in Berlin. The legacy of his philosophy reverberated through the centuries, influencing British Idealism, existentialism, Marxism, and fascism. Philosophers continue to advance Hegel's ideas to this day.

More Quotes From
Georg Wilhelm Friedrich Hegel

"Philosophy must indeed recognize the possibility that the people rise to it, but must not lower itself to the people."

"The objects of philosophy, it is true, are upon the whole the same as those of religion.

In both the object is Truth, in that supreme sense in which God and God only is the Truth."

"The force of mind is only as great as its expression; its depth only as deep as its power to expand and lose itself."

"Discord which appears at first to be a lamentable breach and dissolution of the unity of a party, is really the crowning proof of its success."

"History, is a conscious, self-meditating process—Spirit emptied out into Time."

"What is reasonable is real; that which is real is reasonable."

"What experience and history teach is this— that nations and governments have never learned anything from history, or acted upon any lessons they might have drawn from it."

"It is easier to discover a deficiency in individuals, in states, and in providence, than to see their real import or value."

"*Haste in every business brings failures.*"

—Herodotus

Herodotus

Often described as the world's first historian, Herodotus wrote about the events of his time.

When Herodotus penned his *Histories*, it was the first time a historian had ever approached the documentation of significant events in an investigative manner. Herodotus attempted to collect accounts of historical events from reliable witnesses, and practically invented the concept of using a primary source for a historical record. At the time, his approach represented a major shift from the time-honored Homeric tradition of passing

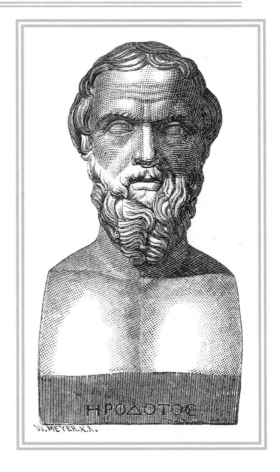

ΗΡΟΔΟΤΟΣ

W.MEYER.X.A.

down epic poems that recounted fantastic events. Because of his method, and the scope of his historical record of the ancient world, Herodotus is often called "the Father of History."

Ironically, very little is known about Herodotus' own life. He was born in the ancient Persian city Halicarnassus—modern day Bodrum, Turkey—on or about the year 484 BCE. By his own eyewitness accounts, Herodotus travelled extensively throughout the ancient world, first visiting Egypt, then through Tyre, and eventually Babylon. No one knows where he eventually settled and died, although it may have been in Athens or Macedonia, sometime around 430 BCE.

During Herodotus' travels, he collected accounts of historical events in the ancient world. His *Histories* are the major source of our understanding of the rise of the Persian Empire and the causes and outcome of the Greek and Persian Wars of the fifth century. He described the events leading up to the Trojan War, and he provided the primary account of the Battle of Thermopylae and other important battles of the Greco-Persian Wars.

Herodotus' wide-ranging *Histories* were not limited to war and politics. He also described the cultures of the ancient world, and gathered local folktales and ancient myths. In one, he recounts the tale of Arion, a musician who brought the *dithyramb*, an ancient hymn that honors Dionysus, to Corinth. Herodotus tells the story of how Arion was captured by pirates on his return from a musical competition in Sicily. Given the choice between suicide and being thrown into the sea, he asked permission to sing a final song, which, according to Herodotus, attracted a pod of dolphins. When he was thrown into the sea, one of the dolphins carried Arion to safety.

On his travels through Egypt, Herodotus reported on its geography and natural history, compiling lists of its local flora and fauna and describing the seasonal flooding of the Nile River. He listed its ancient kings and described the Great Pyramid and the Labyrinth of Egypt, as well as the funeral rites, religious practices, and cuisine of Egypt.

The *Histories* were eventually divided into nine books, each named after one of the Greek muses for literature, science, and the arts.

More Quotes From Herodotus

"In peace, children inter their parents; war violates the order of nature and causes parents to inter their children."

"If a man insisted always on being serious, and never allowed himself a bit of fun and relaxation, he would go mad or become unstable without knowing it."

"It is the gods' custom to bring low all things of surpassing greatness."

"Great deeds are usually wrought at great risks."

"It is better to be envied than pitied."

> *Take time to deliberate; but when the time for action arrives, stop thinking and go in.*

Andrew Jackson

Jackson, Andrew

Andrew Jackson lived a lifetime of striking when the iron was hot and getting tasks done while the opportunity presented itself, ascending from the squalor of his upbringing into the seat of the nation. He fought in defense of this newly sovereign country in the War of 1812, and he saw his campaign against the Second Bank of the United States as a battle for the common man against the privileged few.

Born to Scotch-Irish immigrants in a backwoods region of the Carolinas, Andrew Jackson was the first "self-made man" to reach the White House. With his Scottish Brogue accent and reputation for killing men in duels, he was an unlikely pick for a position previously reserved for gentlemen of distinguished heritage.

It was Jackson's command of the American forces in the most famous battle of his era, the successful defense of New Orleans in the War of 1812, that earned him nationwide acclaim and adoration. His status as a war hero nearly won him the presidency in 1824, but despite Jackson's greater share of the vote, the House of Representatives chose to give the office to John Quincy Adams. The ensuing outrage fueled his 1828 campaign, and he became the nation's seventh president the following year.

The central feature of Jackson's presidency was his crusade against the Second Bank of the United States. Although technically a private corporation, the bank wielded enormous power, functioning as a government-sponsored monopoly against which no state institutions could compete. Jackson, who favored small government and saw himself as the representative of the common man, viewed the bank as an unholy alliance between political favoritism and privileged economic interests.

The Bank's charter was set to expire in 1836, but its president Nicholas Biddle decided to petition for extension in 1832, thinking that in an election year Jackson would avoid drastic action. This turned out to be a major miscalculation, as Jackson's "Bank Veto Message" became the most famous statement of his administration.

Jackson crafted his message to appeal not to Congress but to the larger populace. For every section of the voting public, he had a complaint against the bank to suit their political perspective. The Bank, he said, did have some usefulness but not in its proposed form. He claimed it violated state's rights, was an elitist institution, and catered to foreign interests.

In fact the message addressed so many different perspectives that it contradicted itself many times over. So incoherent was the argument that Biddle took it upon himself to distribute thirty-thousand copies of the statement, thinking it would discredit Jackson altogether.

Again, Biddle miscalculated. The public rallied to Jackson's cry, and he easily won his bid for reelection in 1832. Unfortunately, the veto contributed to a drastic economic downturn culminating in the Panic of 1837, but that problem was left to the succeeding administration.

More Quotes From Andrew Jackson

"The brave man inattentive to his duty, is worth little more to his country, than the coward who deserts her in the hour of danger."

"Desperate courage makes One a majority."

> *Don't mind anything anyone tells you about anyone else. Judge everyone and everything for yourself.*

Henry James

James, Henry

If, as he said, "it takes a great deal of history to produce a little literature," Henry James must have hoarded history like few before or since. Over a long and prolific writing career, he elevated the short story as an art form and gave the world a compelling snapshot of life in America.

The son and namesake of a prominent lecturer and younger brother of philosopher William James, Henry was born in New York in 1843. While William was outgoing, Henry was more introverted: a bookworm, some said. Both boys were taken overseas to learn under governesses and tutors as young children, though they also spent considerable time in Manhattan. Subsequent years in Rhode Island and Boston gave Henry an awareness and love of New England that would later be reflected in his writing.

Extremely bright, James enrolled in Harvard Law School at age nineteen but spent only one year there. Law was not his passion. Books were. He occupied his time reading authors like Nathaniel Hawthorne and Charles Augustin Sainte-Beuve, and writing his own tales as well. By 1865 the prestigious *Atlantic Monthly* was publishing his stories. The editor, William Dean Howells, became a friend of Henry's and together they are credited for ushering in the era of American Realism.

Transatlantic Experience

Steeped in an understanding of Europe that few young American writers could match thanks to his childhood experiences, James continued to travel abroad, visiting England, France, and Italy in 1869. By this time, the twenty-six-year-old was already recognized among the best short story writers in the U.S.

He returned to Massachusetts and finished his first novel, *Watch and Ward*, though he called *Roderick Hudson* his debut five years later. Beginning with the latter, James made his mark by writing about America, and the innocence of the "New World" compared to the corruption of the "Old." *Roderick Hudson* depicted an American sculptor struggling with his artistic passions and personal relationships while in Italy.

Through books like *Roderick Hudson, The American,* and *Daisy Miller* over the next few years, readers all over the world were immersed in the American spirit and to life in the United States and to the adventures of American characters abroad. James also wrote about social reform in 1880s novels *The Bostonians* and *The Princess Casamassima*.

Over fifty-one years of writing, James produced twenty novels, more than one hundred short stories, a dozen plays, and countless quantities of reviews, travel pieces, and articles. More than perhaps anyone before him, he elevated the stature of the short story, gripping readers with fascinating tales and accessible characters, while also showing the kind of craftsmanship that also ranked him among the great American novelists.

James penned three of his most masterful novels later in his life, producing *The Ambassadors, The Wings of the Dove* and *The Golden Bowl* in the first few years of the twentieth century. He had been living in Europe for more than twenty years by this time. James returned to New York in 1905 for the first time in more than a quarter century and edited a New York edition of his selected works.

James spent most of his final years in England. He became a British subject in 1915, received the Order of Merit from King George V in 1916 and died just weeks later in London.

More Quotes From Henry James

"True happiness, we are told, consists in getting out of one's self; but the point is not only to get out—you must stay out; and to stay out you must have some absorbing errand."

"In the long run an opinion often borrows credit from the forbearance of its patrons."

> *It is perfectly true, as the philosophers say, that life must be understood backwards. But they forget the other proposition, that it must be lived forwards.*
>
> *S. Kierkegaard.*

Kierkegaard, Søren

To Kierkegaard, truth was subjective, Christianity was personal, and God was infinite. His work has influenced Western thought well into the twenty-first century.

Søren Kierkegaard was born in Copenhagen, Denmark, on May 5, 1813, to a well-to-do family. Kierkegaard read extensively as a young man, exploring classical and contemporary philosophy as well as plays. He often wandered the streets of Copenhagen, lost in thought. In 1830 he began attending the School of Civic Virtue, and later studied theology at the University of Copenhagen. He began keeping journals while in university, and they grew to some seven-thousand pages by the end of his life. His journals provide a great deal of insight about the development of Kierkegaard's philosophy, although he also published widely. He successfully defended his dissertation in 1841, which discussed irony as it related to the works of Socrates.

Philosophy and Early Writing

In 1842 Kierkegaard wrote the first of many treatises on religion, *De Omnibus Dubitandum Est* (*Everything Must Be Doubted*). In it he discussed the existential problems that arise from the Cartesian system of applying rational skepticism to all things. Kierkegaard followed *Omnibus* with two other books that explored these themes, *Philosophical Fragments* and *Concluding Unscientific Postscript*. In 1843 he anonymously published his first work, *Either/Or*, a two-volume magnum opus on the development of human consciousness. He argues that consciousness begins as a form that is essentially hedonistic, and develops into one that values ethics and morality. The work is presented as two views of life: the first is the aesthetic view, which values beauty and seduction, and the second is the ethical view, which values critical discourse and moral responsibility. *Either/Or* established Kierkegaard's reputation as a writer and philosopher.

Existentialism and Christendom

Kierkegaard continued to publish anonymously during the 1840s, writing a series of *Upbuilding Discourses* that began as two essays and eventually grew to eighteen over the course of a decade. The *Discourses* are written to help improve (or "upbuild") the reader's thinking rather than tear it down, and deal with ethics, morality, love, and religion. He published *Fear and Trembling* and *Repetition* in 1843; in them, he laid the foundations of Existentialist thought. Although Kierkegaard never used the word "existentialism" in his work, he is considered one of the founders of the movement. He argued that human experience, and by extension truth, was inherently subjective, in sharp contrast to the objectivity of mathematics and science. Kierkegaard thought that objective study was too removed from the human experience to be able to approach truth. He used the "Knight of Faith" to illustrate his ideas in these works. This individual is one whose faith in himself and God grants him the freedom to act independently from the world.

In *Works of Love*, published in 1847, he explores the concept of agape love. Agape, or charitable love, which stems from the ancient Greeks, was considered the highest form of love, as compared to erotic love and familial love. *Works of Love* relies heavily on Existentialist arguments to make its case. In his later years Kierkegaard attacked the Lutheran Church in his writing. He criticized Bishop Jacob Peter Mynster after his death, arguing that his ideas about Christianity were incorrect, and that Mynster's theology did not ask enough from Christians. Mynster had been lauded as a "truth-witness" following his death, and Kierkegaard vehemently contested the characterization. He published his criticism in a series of pamphlets called *The Moment*.

Kierkegaard collapsed in the street in October of 1855. He lingered in a hospital bed for a month, before dying on November 11.

More Quotes From Søren Kierkegaard

"What the age needs is not a genius—it has had geniuses enough, but a martyr, who in order to teach men to obey would himself be obedient unto death. What the age needs is awakening. And therefore someday, not only my writings but my whole life, all the intriguing mystery of the machine will be studied and studied. I never forget how God helps me and it is therefore my last wish that everything may be to his honour."

"But on the other hand, the understanding, reflection, is also a gift of God. What shall one do with it, how dispose of it if one is not to use it? And if one then uses it in fear and trembling not for one's own advantage but to serve the truth, if one uses it that way in fear and trembling and furthermore believing that it still is God who determines the issue in its eternal significance, venturing to trust in him, and with unconditional obedience yielding to what he makes use of it: is this not fear of God and serving God the way a person of reflection can, in the somewhat different way than the spontaneously immediate person, but perhaps more ardently."

"The tyrant dies and his rule is over; the martyr dies and his rule begins."

> *A leader is best when people barely know that he exists, not so good when people obey and acclaim him, worst when they despise him. Fail to honor people, They fail to honor you. But of a good leader, who talks little, when his work is done, his aims fulfilled, they will all say, 'We did this ourselves.'*
>
> —Lao-Tzu

Lao-Tzu

Born sometime in the sixth century BCE during the Zhou Dynasty, Lao-Tzu (or Laozi, "Old Master") founded the Chinese philosophy Taoism. Very little is known about Lao-Tzu's life, but his teachings and philosophy have persisted for centuries and remain influential in China and throughout the modern world.

Most of what is known about Lao-Tzu's life is apocryphal, and many legends surround the circumstances of his birth and life. According to legend, he was born after spending eight or eighty years in his mother's womb, and he lived to be 129 years old.

The *Shiji*, a biography of Lao-Tzu written by Sima Qian in 145 BCE, provides much of what we know about him. According to the *Shiji*, Lao-Tzu was born in the Henan Province, and had the family name Li. During the Zhou Dynasty, he was a historian and archivist at the royal court. It was around this time that he met Confucius, who found him fascinating. Lao-Tzu on the other hand criticized the philosopher's arrogance.

Later in life, upon observing the decline of the Zhou Dynasty, Lao-Tzu travelled west to live out his days as a hermit on the frontier. As he travelled through the Xiangu pass, a sentry named Yinxi asked him to write a book of his teachings. The resulting book is said to be the *Tao Te Ching* (*Way of Virtue*). Yinxi became his disciple and they left the pass together.

The *Tao*

The *Tao Te Ching*, or more simply the *Tao* or "The Way," is along with the *Zhuangzi*, one of the two major works of Taoist philosophy. The *Tao* describes the teachings of Taoism with eighty-one short poems. The teachings are divided into descriptions of the philosophical and religious aspects of Taoism. The teachings emphasize *wu wei*, or "effortless action," simplicity, sincerity, and spontaneity. There are three basic virtues in Taoism, called the Three Treasures or the Three Jewels. In the *Tao*, they are described as compassion, frugality, and humility, although later interpretations took them to also mean *jing* (the essence of the physical body), *qi* (life force, including emotions), and *shen* (the spirit).

Lao-Tzu highlighted the significance of nature in the *Tao* and preached that human lives would be enriched by a return to it. The work discusses the primitive state of all existence and heavily discusses the concept of naturalness at length. Lao-Tzu promoted a limited government and urged humility and restraint in leadership, and urged detachment from desires and leading a simple life.

Taoism most heavily influenced the Han Dynasty, during which Lao-Tzu was elevated to a nearly godlike status. This gave rise to the *Tianshi Dao* or "Way of the Celestial Masters' in the second century CE. The movement eventually gained power in the Sichuan state during that time. Eventually, Lao-Tzu came to be considered a personification of the *Tao*, which is described as natural, spontaneous, eternal, nameless, and indescribable.

Lao-Tzu's influence is incredibly widespread, and is, with Confucianism, one of the foundations of Chinese philosophy, but the *Tao* also has heavily influenced many Western philosophers, political scientists, and economists, and many of Lao-Tzu's adages from the *Tao* have been adopted as maxims around the world.

Quotes From Lao-Tzu

"When the people of the world all know beauty as beauty, there arises the recognition of ugliness. When they all know the good as good, there arises the recognition of evil."

"He who loves the world as his body may be entrusted with the empire."

"Manifest plainness. Embrace simplicity. Reduce selfishness. Have few desires."

> *It is easier to be wise for others than for oneself.*
>
> —François

La Rouchefoucald, François de

François VI, or François de La Rouchefoucald, was a French nobleman and writer who mastered the *maxime*, of which he wrote more than five hundred. These epigrams explore difficult or paradoxical truths, and François wrote them with unparalleled eloquence.

François was born in Paris on September 15, 1613, to a noble family at a time when Louis XIV was alternately attacking the French nobility and courting their support. François married Andrée de Vivone in 1628 and joined the army when he was sixteen to fight in the Franco-Spanish War. His family, like many nobles of the day, fell in and out of favor with the monarchy. François participated in a plot against Cardinal Richelieu, Louis XIV's head minister, which resulted in him being imprisoned in the Bastille for eight days and exiled for two years. He participated in the second Fronde, an uprising of the nobility against the Crown, in 1648. The Royal forces and rebels were at war until 1653; François was wounded in the head at the battle of Faubourg Saint-Antoine in 1652 and retired to his family's estate.

In the late 1650s, Madeleine de Souvré, a noted writer, formed a *salon*, or gathering of like-minded literary figures, and invited François to join. It was at this salon that Francois began writing the *Maximes* for which he would become famous. The *Maximes* firmly established his reputation as a man of letters among the French elites. He also corresponded extensively, particularly with the Comtesse de La Fayette, who wrote one of the first novels in history. His *Letters*, along with his *Memoirs*, provide a glimpse of the life of French nobility in the seventeenth century. He died in Paris on March 17, 1680.

More Quotes From François

"Our virtues are most frequently but vices in disguise."

"Self-love is the greatest of all flatterers."

"What we term virtues are often but a mass of various actions and diverse interests, which fortune or our own industry manage to arrange; and it is not always from valour or from chastity that men are brave, and women chaste."

"Passion often renders the most clever man a fool, and even sometimes renders the most foolish man clever."

"We all have strength enough to endure the misfortunes of others."

"Philosophy triumphs easily over past and future evils; but present evils triumph over it."

"Neither the sun nor death can be looked at steadily."

"If we had no faults, we should not take so much pleasure in noting those of others."

"We promise according to our hopes; we fulfill according to our fears."

"Those who apply themselves too much to little things often become incapable of great ones."

"To succeed in the world we do everything we can to appear successful already."

> *All things will be clear and distinct to the man who does not hurry; haste is blind and improvident.*
>
> —Livy

Livius, Titus "Livy"

Without Livy, the rise of the Roman Republic and triumphs of its people may have been lost to history.

Livy was born in Patavium (modern-day Padua) around 59 BCE, and was formally educated there. He began writing brief philosophical and historical works at a young age. While little is known of his personal life, he did marry and had a small family. At the age of thirty, Livy travelled to Rome, where he would gain fame as a historian.

Livy's most famous work, *Ab Urbe Condita* (*From the Foundation of the City*), was a 142-volume history of the Roman Republic, covering a period of seven centuries from the founding of Rome through the collapse of the Republic and the beginning of the Imperial period and reign of Caesar Augusts.

Only a fraction of the Condita survives, but the portion that does remain provides a fascinating picture of the rise of the Republic. In it, Livy described at length what he considered the downfall of the Roman character, and the work heavily emphasized a Stoic philosophy and ethical outlook. Livy believed that historical works should elevate as well as inform the reader.

The remainder of his work is mostly lost, although there are brief summaries of most of his writings. Livy was on familiar terms with the Emperor Octavian (Augustus), and is said to have encouraged the future Emperor Claudius to study history when he was young.

He returned to Patavium in his old age, and is believed to have died there in CE 17, a few years after the death of Augustus.

More Quotes From Livy

"We can endure neither our vices nor the remedies for them."

"This above all makes history useful and desirable: it unfolds before our eyes a glorious record of exemplary actions."

"Shared danger is the strongest of bonds; it will keep men united in spite of mutual dislike and suspicion."

"From abundance springs satiety."

"Better late than never."

Reading furnishes the mind only with materials of knowledge; it is thinking that makes what we read ours.

John Locke

Locke, John

John Locke was one of the most significant philosophers in seventeenth century England. His ideas about government revolutionized Western ideas about politics, and influenced the revolutions of the eighteenth century.

John Locke was born on August 29, 1632, in Somerset, England. His parents were Puritans and Locke was raised in that faith. His father was a lawyer, and Locke received an excellent education. He attended Westminster School in London, and enrolled in Christ Church, Oxford, in 1652, where he studied metaphysics, Latin, and Greek. He graduated in 1656, returning in 1658 for a Master of Arts. Following graduate school, he took on a teaching job at Oxford. Some years later Locke would receive a bachelor's of medicine from Oxford as well. He was inducted into the Royal Society in 1668.

Locke's landmark work, *Two Treatises of Government*, was published anonymously in 1689. His ideas about the natural rights of man and the social contract were groundbreaking at the time, and laid the foundations for much of the philosophy of the eighteenth century. Locke's *Two Treatises* significantly influenced Thomas Jefferson, John Adams, and many of the other leaders of the American Revolution, and also inspired the French Revolution.

After an attempt on the life of King Charles II that became known as the Rye House Plot, Locke fell out of the good graces of the government, in spite of the fact that he was most likely not involved. He was forced to flee to Holland. While there, he wrote *An Essay Concerning Human Understanding*, which was as groundbreaking as his *Two Treatises*. The work spanned four volumes and explored the nature of human knowledge. Following the Glorious Revolution of 1688, Locke was able to return to England. He spent his final years in Essex, where he died on October 28, 1704.

More Quotes From John Locke

"To love truth for truth's sake is the principal part of human perfection in this world, and the seed-plot of all other virtues."

"New opinions are always suspected, and usually opposed, without any other reason but because they are not already common."

"I have always thought the actions of men the best interpreters of their thoughts."

> ❝ *A prudent man should always follow in the path trodden by great men and imitate those who are most excellent.* ❞

Machiavelli, Niccolo

A sixteenth century diplomat, philosopher, humanist, and the author of one of the most influential books on political philosophy, Niccolo Machiavelli is considered the father of political science.

Niccolo di Bernardo dei Machiavelli was born in Florence, Italy, in 1469, the son of an attorney. At the time of his birth, Italy was still divided into four competing city-states, and the powerful Medici family had ruled Florence for sixty years. During this tumultuous time in the country's history, various European powers, including France, Spain, Switzerland, and the Holy Roman Empire routinely invaded Italy and captured city-states as they vied for regional dominance.

In 1494 a rebellion established the Florentine Republic and expelled the Medici family. Machiavelli was appointed a diplomat of the Republic, and took several missions to the Vatican in Rome. His diplomatic experience to Rome and Spain would later influence his political philosophy in *The Prince*. In 1512 the Medici, with the support of the Vatican, recaptured Florence and abolished the Republic. Machiavelli was jailed for three weeks and tortured to discover if he had any role in the conspiracy of 1494. He denied any involvement, and was released, but forbidden from participating in politics.

Writing *The Prince*

Machiavelli returned to his country estate after his imprisonment, and immersed himself in writing and study. Initially a dark time in his career, Machiavelli's exile from politics would ultimately give him the time to develop his political philosophy and write the political treatises that would become *The Prince* and other works. *The Prince* has themes of self-determination in the face of the power of fate, and advances the political philosophy that ruthlessness and ambition are acceptable means to establish and maintain total authority. It is widely considered a manual for politicians on how to employ cunning and deceit in self-serving capacities, and gave rise to the pejorative term "Machiavellian" to describe someone who does so. The title character was likely inspired by Cesare Borgia, the illegitimate son of Pope Alexander VI whose ruthless fight for power Machiavelli witnessed firsthand while he was a diplomat in Rome.

The Prince discusses the politics of princedoms as well as republics, and the first part deals with "new" and "mixed" (parts of an older established state) princedoms. The second part of the book discusses the ways people can rise to power, according to Machiavelli. The first way is by their own virtue, which he sees as difficult, but resulting in a stable and respected position of power. The second is by the blessing of the existing regime, in which power is easier to attain but harder to keep. The third is by "criminal virtue," such as assassination or bribery; Machiavelli advises that if one wishes to attain power in this manner, they should execute their nefarious plans all at once, so that they do not run the risk of having to continually commit more wicked acts to maintain power. The fourth way one can come to power is by the selection of one's fellow citizens, either by those who want to command the people through the ruler, or by the people themselves. Each has its own merits and pitfalls.

In addition to *The Prince* Machiavelli wrote *The Discourses on Livy, On the Art of War*, a series of histories of Florence, and a number of poems and plays, including *The Mandrake*, a satirical criticism of the House of Medici. Machiavelli died in Florence on June 21, 1527, and was buried in the church of Santa Croce.

More Quotes From Machiavelli

"The chief foundations of all states, new as well as old or composite, are good laws and good arms."

"A prince should therefore have no other aim or thought, nor take up any other thing for his study, but war and its organization

and discipline, for that is the only art that is necessary to one who commands."

"Among other evils which being unarmed brings you, It causes you to be despised."

"A prince being thus obliged to know well how to act as a beast must imitate the fox and the lion, for the lion cannot protect himself from traps, and the fox cannot defend himself from wolves. One must therefore be a fox to recognize traps, and a lion to frighten wolves."

"Where the willingness is great, the difficulties cannot be great."

"He who believes that new benefits will cause great personages to forget old injuries is deceived."

"It is the nature of men to be bound by the benefits they confer as much as by those they receive."

"He who builds on the people, builds on the mud."

> ## *We cannot live only for ourselves. A thousand fibers connect us with our fellow men.*
>
> —Herman Melville

Melville, Herman

Herman Melville was at a crossroads in 1850. The thirty-one-year-old New Yorker had enjoyed success with his debut novel, *Typee*, a few years earlier but was struggling to produce a manuscript he had promised about a whaler on the South Seas. He had buried an older brother and married Elizabeth Shaw a few years earlier. He was writing, but his efforts lacked inspiration.

But then, in the summer of 1850, his focus and drive came back to his writing. Melville and a group of writers embarked on a climb of Monument Mountain in Massachusetts. It was there he met New Englander Nathanial Hawthorne, of *The Scarlet Letter* fame, and the two quickly became close. In fact, Melville bought a farm in Massachusetts and moved his family there so he and Hawthorne could be neighbors.

The vigor having returned to his craft, Melville finished what started out as *The Whale* and became *Moby Dick.* The tale of Ishmael, Ahab, and a great white whale became one of the true American classics. *The Oxford Companion to English Literature* calls the book "the closest approach the United States has had to a national prose epic."

The fibers that connected Melville with his fellow man— Hawthorne, in this case—came along at just the right time. Melville continued writing until just a few years before his death in 1891. He turned away from the novel in favor of poetry in his later years.

Though he gained popularity in the mid-nineteenth century, it was not until twenty to thirty years after his death that Melville enjoyed a critical revival as his works were revisited and his name ascended near the top of the list of great American writers.

More Quotes From Herman Melville

"Not one man in five cycles, who is wise, will expect appreciative recognition from his fellows, or any one of them."

"In me divine magnanimities are spontaneous and instantaneous—catch them while you can."

"Leviathan is not the biggest fish; —I have heard of Krakens."

"It is—or seems to be—a wise sort of thing, to realise that all that happens to a man in this life is only by way of joke, especially his misfortunes, if he have them. And it is also worth bearing in mind, that the joke is passed round pretty liberally & impartially, so that not very many are entitled to fancy that they in particular are getting the worst of it."

"Whoever is not in the possession of leisure can hardly be said to possess independence. They talk of the dignity of work. Bosh. True Work is the necessity of poor humanity's earthly condition. The dignity is in leisure."

"Familiarity with danger makes a brave man braver, but less daring."

"It is better to fail in originality, than to succeed in imitation. He who has never failed somewhere, that man can not be great. Failure is the true test of greatness."

> ## *"Never has a man who has bent himself been able to make others straight.*
>
> —Mencius

Mencius

Born nearly a century after Confucius, Mencius (or Mengzi, "Master Meng") would eventually become known as "The Second Sage" for his contributions to Confucianism.

Mencius collated and interpreted Confucius' teachings, and helped form them into a comprehensive philosophy to which he added his own ideas and teachings. Like Confucius, little is known about Mencius' life, although the biographer Sima Qian, who also wrote about Confucius, said he was born in Lu in northeast China during the Warring States Period following the collapse of the Zhou Dynasty.

Mencius is best known for is his belief that human nature is inherently good, a concept he called *xing shan*. He taught that a characteristic of a person can be part of the person's nature even if it is not expressed. For example, bearing fruit is a characteristic of orange trees. Even if most orange seeds do not develop into trees that bear fruit, Mencius said, they retain the characteristic as part of their nature. Like an orange seed, he taught that with education and self-discipline, human goodness can be cultivated. With negative influences or neglect it can be wasted, but it remains an inherent part of human nature.

He also proposed the idea of The Four Sprouts, in which negative reactions can lead to positive outcomes because of human goodness. Feeling pity, for example, will grow to humanity, as feeling shame will grow to righteousness.

Mencius' writings eventually became the core philosophy of orthodox Confucianism.

More Quotes From Mencius

"The great man is the one who does not lose his child's heart."

"He who exerts his mind to the utmost knows his nature."

"If the king loves music, there is little wrong in the land."

"The way of learning is none other than finding the lost mind."

It is better to be Socrates dissatisfied than a pig satisfied.

J. S. Mill

Mill, John Stuart

Promoting the happiness of all sentient beings was the highest form of ethics, according to Mill.

John Stuart Mill was born in London on May 20, 1806. His father, a philosopher and historian, played a large role in his early education. Mill began learning Greek when he was three years old, and Latin when he was eight. By the time he was a teenager, Mill had a strong background in world history, logic, and economic theory. When he was fourteen, he travelled to France for a year, and stayed at the home of the mechanical engineer Samuel Bentham. On his return, his father used his connections at the British East India Company to secure a job for him. Eventually Mill would replace his father as a chief examiner at the company.

Mill suffered a nervous breakdown and fell into a deep depression in 1826. The "mental crisis," as he would later describe it, was brought on by the demands his father placed on him, but it would have a beneficial outcome. While he was struggling with his depression, Mill began to reconsider the validity of some of the philosophy his father and Samuel Bentham had taught him. He began reading the poetry of William Wordsworth, which he found relaxing, and as he came out of his depression he left much of his old ideas behind.

Harriet Taylor and Major Works

In 1830 he became friends with Harriet Taylor, a philosopher and feminist writer. They collaborated on many of the works Mill would go on to publish under his own name. The two exchanged essays on women's rights, marriage, and philosophy. When Taylor's husband died in 1851, she and Mill married. They continued to work together until she died in 1858. Harriet's daughter Helen continued to work with Mill for fifteen years following her mother's death.

In 1830 John Herschel published a work on natural philosophy that argued that laws were self-evident truths. Several luminaries continued to expand on his work for the next decade. In 1843 Mill published his first major work, *A System of Logic*, which opposed Herschel's work, arguing that laws could be deduced by inductive logic and observation. Mill's next major work, *On Liberty*, would not be published until 1859. It was Mill's landmark work, arguing for individual freedom from the government and society. Mills argued that people should not be constrained in their behavior or beliefs by either the law or social mores. Four years later, he would follow it with *Utilitarianism*, which was published initially as a series of essays. It would be his most famous work.

Utilitarianism discusses much of Bentham's philosophy, and in it he offers his "greatest happiness principle." This argues that one's actions should be designed to promote the happiness of as many sentient beings as possible. The "rightness" of an action can be measured by the amount of happiness it produces. Any code of ethics that arose from such a standard would be easy to internalize, and therefore naturally spread itself.

In 1869 Mill wrote *The Subjection of Women*, in which he argues for women's suffrage and equal education. This was a very controversial position for a man to take at the time, and he was subjected to some ridicule because of it. While he was initially in favor of a free market, he also supported labor unions and farming cooperatives as his philosophy began to take on a more socialist inclination, perhaps in part due to Harriet Taylor's influence.

Mill died on May 8, 1873, in Avignon, France.

More Quotes From John Stuart Mill

"The best state for human nature is that in which, while no one is poor, no one desires to be richer, nor has any reason to fear being thrust back by the efforts of others to push themselves forward."

"It is not because men's desires are strong that they act ill; it is because their consciences are weak."

"How can great minds be produced in a country where the test of a great mind is agreeing in the opinions of small minds?"

"France has done more for even English history than England has."

"The only purpose for which power can be rightfully exercised over any member of a civilized community, against his will, is to prevent harm to others. His own good, either physical or moral, is not a sufficient warrant."

> *If you want a golden rule that will fit everybody, this is it: Have nothing in your houses that you do not know to be useful, or believe to be beautiful.*
>
> —William Morris

Morris, William

From home design to literature to politics, William Morris operated with a discerning eye and an exquisite touch. Associated with the Pre-Raphaelite Brotherhood and the English Arts and Crafts movement, he campaigned for Great Britain's nineteenth century socialist movement.

William Morris was born in 1834 in Essex, England, the son of a prominent financier. As a child, he was a voracious reader and was also interested in gardening, practicing on his family's sprawling grounds. His early ambitions were architecture and painting. Morris attended Oxford, where he became inspired by the medieval architecture. He was drawn to middle age values like chivalry and community.

Morris met lifelong friend and collaborator Edward Burne-Jones while both were in their first year at Oxford. Along with other aspiring young artists and thinkers like Richard Watson Dixon and Charles Faulkner, their "brotherhood" would meet regularly to debate, recite Shakespeare, and discuss politics and art.

Morris took an architectural apprenticeship in London after earning his BA but began to tire of architecture. He met and became close friends with Dante Gabriel Rossetti, one of the most prominent pre-Raphaelite painters, and through Rossetti also became acquainted with others producing what he considered to be world-changing art.

Around the same time he was deciding to give up architecture for painting and poetry, Morris met Jane Burden at a theater performance and, in 1859, married her despite her working-class upbringing. He commissioned an architect friend, Philip Webb, to build them a home in Kent. Morris wanted a modern home that was "medieval in spirit." Webb obliged, and Morris and his wife moved into Red House in 1860.

Passion for Design

The Red House proved to be the inspiration for what Morris would become—one of the foremost names in textile design.

With help from his friends, he spent the better part of two years decorating and furnishing the home. Their gifts for design were obvious, so they decided in 1861 to turn their passion into a business: Morris, Marshall, Faulkner & Co. They began producing furniture, tableware, embroidery, stained glass, tiles, and other home furnishings. Morris could not find any wallpaper he liked, so wallpaper design became another staple of the business.

The impact of their business extended far beyond Red House. Homes and churches all over England began turning to Morris and his colleagues, who started calling themselves "The Firm." They showcased their work at the 1862 International Exhibition in South Kensington and soon found themselves in high demand. Their designs continued to influence décor in homes and churches well into the twentieth century.

Morris left no stone unturned in the design industry, which he considered art. He took up dyeing and weaving textiles, coming up with new designs and eschewing chemical dyes in favor of organic ones. He became politically active, at one point embracing Marxism and founding the Socialist League in 1884.

While most of his greatest contributions came in the area of home design and décor, Morris continued to paint and write throughout his life. He published several collections of poetry and fiction, translated ancient and medieval works and founded the Kelmscott Press in 1891. Its 1896 edition of the *Works of Geoffrey Chaucer*—put out the year Morris died—is widely recognized as a masterpiece in book design.

> *Between every two pine trees there is a door leading to a new way of life.*
> —John Muir

Muir, John

John Muir was perhaps the most influential conservationist in the history of the United States. A farmer, naturalist, and prolific writer, Muir's tireless efforts to protect America's natural resources led to the creation of the National Parks System. He is often called "John of the Mountains" or the "Father of the National Parks."

John Muir was born in Scotland on April 21, 1838. When he was eleven, his family immigrated to the United States, settling in Wisconsin. Muir worked on his family farm until he attended the University of Wisconsin at twenty-two. After three years, he left school to explore the northwest United States and Canada, supporting himself with odd jobs. In 1867, while he was working in a wagon wheel factory, he was injured and nearly lost his sight. Upon recovering, he determined to follow his dream of wandering the natural spaces of the nation.

At Home Outdoors

He first undertook a thousand-mile walk from Indianapolis to Florida. Muir sailed to Cuba, and then to New York, where he booked passage to San Francisco. It was in California that he would find his true home in the Sierra Nevada and Yosemite. Upon seeing Yosemite for the first time in 1868, he was overwhelmed by its pristine valley and soaring mountain peaks. Muir built a small cabin along Yosemite Creek, and lived there for the next two years.

During this time, he explored Yosemite's high country, often alone, carrying nothing but a loaf of bread, a handful of tea, a tin cup, and a copy of Ralph Waldo Emerson's writings. He'd often spend the night sitting in his overcoat next to a campfire, reading Emerson. He was often visited by scientists, naturalists, and artists. In 1871 he was visited by Emerson himself. His hero offered him a teaching position at Harvard on the spot, but Muir declined, later saying he couldn't give up "God's big show" for a professorship.

Muir made four trips to Alaska and the Pacific Northwest over the next ten years, exploring Glacier Bay, Wrangel Island, and climbing Mount Rainer.

Activism and the National Parks

In 1874 Muir published a series of articles about the Sierra Nevada. These were the beginning of a vast collection of hundreds of articles and ten books about the natural world, conservation, and his travels. He married Louisa Strentzel in 1880, and raised a family with her in Martinez, California. But he never stopped travelling, visiting Australia, South America,

Africa, Asia, and Europe, and returning many times to the Sierra Nevada.

In order to protect his beloved Yosemite and promote preservation of natural spaces, Muir co-founded the Sierra Club in 1892. The organization fought to protect the Park from grazing and prevent it from being reduced in size.

In 1889 a series of Muir's articles appeared in *Century* magazine that highlighted the devastation of the meadows and forests of Yosemite by sheep and cattle grazing. Working with *Century's* editor Robert Underwood Johnson, Muir was able to convince Congress to create Yosemite National Park. Muir would eventually be involved in the creation of the Sequoia, Petrified Forest, Grand Canyon, and Mount Rainer National Parks.

In 1901 he published *Our National Parks*, which prompted President Theodore Roosevelt to visit him in Yosemite. Upon entering the park, Roosevelt asked Muir to show him "the real Yosemite," and the two set off alone to hike through the back country. They talked late into the night, and slept under the stars at Glacier Point. The experience, and Muir's advocacy, convinced Roosevelt to create the National Parks Service and put Yosemite and other Parks under Federal protection.

Muir died in Los Angeles on Christmas Eve, 1914.

More Quotes From John Muir

"Bears are made of the same dust as we, and breathe the same winds and drink of the same waters. A bear's days are warmed by the same sun, his dwellings are overdomed by the same blue sky, and his life turns and ebbs with heart-pulsings like ours and was poured from the same fountain."

"Man as he came from the hand of his Maker was poetic in both mind and body, but the gross heathenism of civilization has generally destroyed Nature, and poetry, and all that is spiritual."

"Living artificially in towns, we are sickly, and never come to know ourselves."

"When we try to pick out anything by itself, we find it hitched to everything else in the universe."

> # *Let the man who does not wish to be idle fall in love!*
> —Ovid

Ovid

One of the greatest of the Roman poets, he would live out his days exiled by the Emperor in a remote province on the Black Sea. The exact circumstances surrounding his exile are not clear, but Ovid wrote that it was for "a poem and a mistake."

Born Publius Ovidius Naso in Sulmo, Italy, in 43 BCE, Ovid was educated in rhetoric by Arellius Fuscus in Rome. His father wanted him to pursue a career as a lawyer, but following the death of his brother, Ovid abandoned the law and become a poet instead.

His first of many public recitations was when he was eighteen years old. He would go on to enjoy great success for the next twenty-five years, primarily writing poetry in elegiac style with erotic and romantic themes. Some of his better known works from this period include the *Amores*, a series of erotic poems written to a lover named Corinna, and the *Heroides*, love letters written by mythological heroines. He also wrote the *Ars Amatoria* (*Art of Love*), a three-volume work about seduction that was intended to parody the style of didactic poetry that was popular at the time.

Ovid's most famous and perhaps most ambitious work is the *Metamorphoses*, completed in 8 CE. A fifteen-volume work, it covered the history of Greek and Roman mythology from the creation of the universe to the deification of Julius Caesar in 42 BCE. Ovid describes human beings being transformed into trees, constellations, animals, and flowers in the epic poem.

The same year, he was exiled by Augustus to Tomis, where he would spend the rest of his life. While there, he wrote two collections of poetry that described his depression and loneliness. Ovid died there in 17 or 18 CE.

More Quotes From Ovid

"So I can't live either without you or with you."

"To be loved, be loveable."

"Nothing is stronger than habit."

"Time: the devourer of all things."

"You will be safest in the middle."

"Love is a thing full of anxious fears."

"The result justifies the deed."

Character is much easier kept than recovered.

T. Paine

Paine, Thomas

Thomas Paine was a political writer whose pamphlet *Common Sense* laid the foundations for the American Revolution and convinced the American colonists that the revolution was necessary. He also wrote several other influential treatises on subjects including the French Revolution and religion.

Thomas Paine was born in 1737 in England. His father was a Quaker and his mother was Anglican. He did not receive much schooling, but did learn to read and write. When he was thirteen years old, he joined his father in his trade as a rope maker for ships. After living and working in England for most of his adult life, he sailed to America in 1774, arriving in Philadelphia. In America he immediately began working in publishing, starting as an assistant editor of the *Pennsylvania Magazine*. He began writing his own articles, publishing them under assumed names. One of his earliest political articles attacked the institution of slavery, which he authored under the pseudonym "Justice & Humanity."

Common Sense

Paine had been in Philadelphia only five months when the Revolutionary War broke out at the battles of Lexington and Concord. He realized that the revolt could not merely be a rebellion against the taxes levied by Parliament, but should fight for complete independence from the British crown. He developed this position in a pamphlet fifty pages long that was printed on January 10, 1776. The pamphlet's title was *Common Sense*.

The pamphlet's rhetoric is designed to pressure the reader to choose a side and make a choice on the question of revolution against the Crown. *Common Sense* brilliantly forces the issue of complete independence from Great Britain, showing the reader that the only remedy against tyranny was freedom. The incendiary pamphlet was widely reprinted and distributed throughout the thirteen colonies, and helped stoke revolutionary sentiment among the colonists. Because of it, recruitment by the Continental Army increased, and the colonies found themselves united for the cause of independence.

During the Revolution, Paine travelled with the Continental Army as an attaché to General Nathanael Greene. Between 1776 and 1783, he published a series of sixteen *Crisis Papers*, which encouraged the revolutionary soldiers to remain in the fight regardless of how dire the situation became, and to remember that they were fighting for the virtuous cause of liberty. The first of the *Crisis Papers*, published in December 1776, was read to the troops at Valley Forge to inspire them to persevere through the punishing winter.

After the Revolution

Following the war, Paine was appointed to the Committee for Foreign Affairs in 1777, and held the post until a scandal forced his resignation in 1779. He then served as clerk of the Pennsylvania General Assembly. While there, he wrote *Public Good* in 1780, which called for a Constitutional Convention to replace the Articles of Confederation.

In 1787 he returned to England, and began supporting the French Revolution. When he read an argument against the Revolution, Paine wrote a response in 1791. *The Rights of Man* not only defended the Revolution but went on to and criticize the aristocracy and assail the tradition of inheritance. He was accused of treason and the book was banned, but by then he had already travelled to France.

He returned to America in 1802 at the invitation of President Thomas Jefferson, and lived there until his death in 1809.

More Quotes From Thomas Paine

"Government, even in its best state, is but a necessary evil; in its worst state, an intolerable one."

"What we obtain too cheap, we esteem too lightly."

"Those who expect to reap the blessings of freedom must, like men, undergo the fatigue of supporting it."

"My country is the world and my religion is to do good."

"He who dares not offend cannot be honest."

> *It is man's natural sickness to believe that he possesses the Truth.*
> —Blaise Pascal

Pascal, Blaise

Blaise Pascal was a French mathematician and theological philosopher who discovered many of the foundations of modern probability theory.

Blaise Pascal was born in Clermont-Ferrand, France, on June 19, 1623. His father, a mathematician, educated him at home, recognizing that he was a prodigy at a young age. He initially did not teach Pascal mathematics out of a concern the boy would be so fascinated by

geometry that he would neglect his other studies. But at the age of twelve, Pascal began studying geometry on his own. He began accompanying his father to meetings of mathematicians in Paris, and when he was sixteen, he delivered several of his early theorems to the group. The following year he published

Essay on Conic Sections, and in 1642 he invented a mechanical calculator called the Pascaline, which used a series of wheels to perform calculations.

Pascal began experimenting in the physical sciences in the 1640s, and developed a proof that atmospheric pressure could be measured in terms of weight. He began working on a perpetual motion machine, and while

he was unsuccessful, he accidentally invented the roulette wheel. Around the same time, he began corresponding with the mathematician Pierre de Fermat. The two independently came up with a rudimentary theory of probability.

Pascal's family were Jesuits, having converted in 1646, and he became a religious apologist. His most famous argument for the existence of God, "Pascal's Wager," states that humans bet on God's existence with their own lives. Pascal argued that given what he saw as the infinite rewards for believing in God if God does exist, versus the relatively minor loss from believing if God does not, it is logical to believe in God.

Pascal died on August 19, 1662.

More Quotes From Blaise Pascal

"I made this [letter] very long only because I have not had the leisure to make it shorter."

"People almost invariably arrive at their beliefs not on the basis of proof but on the basis of what they find attractive."

"Do not imagine that it is less an accident by which you find yourself master of the wealth which you possess, than that by which this man found himself king."

"People are generally better persuaded by the reasons which they have themselves discovered than by those which have come into the mind of others."

"I lay it down as a fact that if all men knew what each said of the other, there would not be four friends in the world."

"Nature gives us ... passions and desires suitable to our present state. We are only troubled by the fears which we, and not nature, give ourselves ... "

In the fields of observation chance favours only the prepared mind.

L. Pasteur

Pasteur, Louis

Louis Pasteur's contributions to modern biology
are immense: he discovered pasteurization,
vaccinations for anthrax and rabies, and microbial
fermentation. His discoveries advanced the
germ theory of disease, disproved the theory of
spontaneous generation, and helped to found the
study of bacteriology.

Pasteur was born in Dole, France, in 1822. Although he was
an average student, he obtained a Bachelor of Arts in 1840,
a Bachelor of Science in 1842, and a Doctorate at the École
Normale in Paris in 1847. He spent the first several years of
his career as a teacher and researcher in Dijon Lycée before
becoming a chemistry professor at the University of Strasbourg.
He married Marie Laurent, the daughter of the university's
director, and together they had five children. Three survived to
adulthood.

Chirality and Isomerism

In 1849 Pasteur was studying the chemical properties of tartaric
acid, a crystal found in wine sediments, and comparing them
to paratartaric acid, a synthetic compound which had the same
chemical composition. The two behaved differently, however,
and he determined to discover why. He passed polarized light
through each crystal, and found that while tartaric acid rotated
the light, paratartaric acid did not. In doing so he discovered
the principles of molecular chirality and isomerism; the former
describes compounds that are mirror images, and the latter the

fact that compounds can have identical molecular formulas and different chemical structures.

Fermentation and Germ Theory

In 1856 a winemaker asked Pasteur his advice on preventing stored alcohol from going bad. Pasteur surmised that fermentation and spoiling are caused by microorganisms, and demonstrated that the presence of oxygen was not necessary for this to occur. He showed experimentally that wine soured when

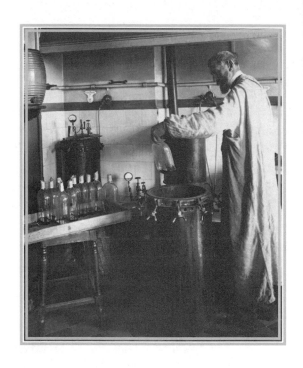

lactic acid was produced by bacterial contamination. Having established this, he then realized that heating liquids could kill the majority of microorganisms that were present, preventing them from spoiling. He patented the process in 1865, calling it pasteurization.

His discovery that bacteria were responsible for fermentation and spoiling led him to suggest that the same microorganisms also caused human and animal diseases—now called the germ theory of disease. He proposed that protecting humans from bacteria could reduce disease, leading to the development of antiseptics.

Disproving Spontaneous Generation

For centuries, the prevailing wisdom held that living organisms arose spontaneously from nonliving matter; fleas were believed to appear from dust and maggots from dead flesh. Pasteur suspected that this was not the case when he observed that yeast did not grow on sterilized grapes. His assertion that spontaneous generation was incorrect sparked a furious debate, and the French Academy of Sciences proposed a cash prize for anyone who could prove or disprove the theory. Pasteur devised an experiment in which he boiled broth in swan-necked flasks. The necks of the flasks prevented airborne particles from reaching the broth. He also exposed a control set of boiled broth to the air. Nothing grew in the swan-necked flasks, but microorganisms did grow in the control set, demonstrating that spontaneous generation was incorrect.

Vaccination

Pasteur discovered the principle of vaccination almost by accident. While he was studying chicken cholera, his assistant inoculated a group of chickens with a culture of the disease that had spoiled. While the chickens became ill, they did not die. Pasteur attempted to re-infect the chickens, but discovered that the weakened culture had made them immune to cholera. Pasteur would go on to apply this principle to developing vaccinations for anthrax and rabies.

He founded the Pasteur Institute in 1887. In 1894 he suffered a stroke, and died the next year. He was buried at Notre Dame Cathedral.

More Quotes From Louis Pasteur

"I am on the edge of mysteries and the veil is getting thinner and thinner."

"There does not exist a category of science to which one can give the name applied science. There are sciences and the applications of science, bound together as the fruit of the tree which bears it."

"Posterity will one day laugh at the foolishness of modern materialistic philosophers."

"Science knows no country, because knowledge belongs to humanity, and is the torch which illuminates the world."

"Science brings men nearer to God."

"A bottle of wine contains more philosophy than all the books in the world."

"The human spirit, driven by an invincible force, will never cease to ask: What is beyond?"

> *Become such as you are, having learned what that is.*
>
> —Pindar

Pindar

A genuine rock star of antiquity, Pindar was one of the most famous of the nine canonical lyric poets of ancient Greece. A large portion of his work was carefully preserved, which may be due to the high regard so many of his peers had for him. Pindar is particularly celebrated for his *epinicia*, victory odes to notable figures and athletes of the day. One could say Pindar popularized the original athletic "fight song."

Pindar was born near the ancient Greek city of Thebes around the year 518. A noble, his family traced their lineage back to the city's founder Cadmus. He began producing poems fairly early on; his oldest existing ode dates from 498 BCE, written when he was just twenty years old. He continued to write poems until he was at least seventy-two years old, although the peak of his work is generally believed to have taken place from about 480 to 460 BCE.

Pindar travelled throughout the Greek world, visiting the royal courts in a number of city-states, which helped spread his reputation far and wide. He visited Syracuse, Delphi, and Athens and wrote odes to many of these cities and their rulers. He became so highly regarded that when Alexander the Great invaded Greece, he ordered his army to spare Pindar's house in Thebes. Pindar had composed complimentary works about Alexander's father, King Alexander I of Macedon.

He is believed to have died in Argos in 443 or 438 BCE.

More Quotes From Pindar

"The days that are still to come are the wisest witnesses."

"Words have a longer life than deeds."

"Not every truth is the better for showing its face undisguised; and often silence is the wisest thing for a man to heed."

> *Never discourage anyone who continually makes progress, no matter how slow.*
>
> —Plato

Plato

Plato was one of the most influential of the ancient Greek philosophers. He founded the famous Academy in Athens, which would devote itself to philosophical and scientific research and education. Plato's extensive works on philosophy, politics and mathematics influenced many of the thinkers of his day and for centuries to come.

Plato's influence on his contemporaries is demonstrated by the fact that he is one of the few ancient philosophers whose works were preserved practically in their entirety. Little is known about his early life,

but it's believed he was born in Athens or Aegina around 428 BCE. Plato died in 348 or 347 BCE.

Plato wrote extensively, but was modest about recording his own life. He may have traveled in the ancient world before returning to Athens at the age of forty, when he founded the Academy. The Academy endured for nearly three centuries until it was destroyed by the Roman general Sulla in 84 BCE.

Plato developed his philosophical ideas and scientific theories at the Academy. He tackled metaphysics in his argument that universal properties exist independently of any mind or description. This idea, called Platonic Realism, started a centuries-long debate about realism that persists in ontological studies today. Plato's Theory of Forms, famously explained in his allegory of the cave, argues that the world as it appears is not real, but merely a "copy" of the real world. And his epistemology (or theory of knowledge) holds that knowledge is intrinsic, and learning is actually recalling innate truths.

In *The Republic* Plato laid out his political theory. In brief, he divided society into three classes: producers and workers, warriors and guardians, and rulers, or philosopher kings. Written in Socratic dialogue, it remains his most famous work.

More Quotes From Plato

"Let every man remind their descendants that they also are soldiers who must not desert the ranks of their ancestors, or from cowardice fall behind."

"All that is said by any of us can only be imitation and representation."

"Friends have all things in common."

"For once touched by love, everyone becomes a poet."

"It is impossible to conceive of many without one."

> *That man is not truly brave who is afraid either to seem or to be, when it suits him, a coward.*

Poe, Edgar Allan

Eccentric at best, misunderstood at worst, and recognized as one of the first American writers to gain worldwide acclaim, Edgar Allan Poe contributed to the growth of several genres during his brief forty years of life. Much of his literature continues to hold sway on university English departments to this day.

"Once upon a midnight dreary," the well-known opening line of "The Raven," could easily describe the early life of

Poe. Poe was born in Boston to two struggling actors in 1809. His father abandoned the family when Edgar was one and his mother died the following year. Sent to Richmond to live with John and Frances Allan (and to take their name), the orphaned Poe tangled with both his foster father and his life in general.

Poe attended the University of Virginia for one semester, enlisted in the U.S. Army under a phony name and could not make it as a West Point cadet. He wanted to be a writer at a time when no one, particularly no one in the U.S., made authoring a fulltime job. The odds were stacked against Poe, but he saw it as game to try.

Poe was twenty-six when he fell in love with his thirteen-year-old cousin, Virginia Clemm, whom he married in 1836. He had enjoyed varying degrees of success with poetry and prose early in his career until making a concerted effort to produce a masterpiece with his poem, "The Raven," in 1845. The tale of a talking raven visiting a mourning narrator resonated with readers due to its themes of love and loss, and its struggle between wanting to hold onto painful sorrow and trying to forget it.

Poe's life would feature more such sorrow. His wife died in 1847, and his drinking and depression worsened. Both have been discussed as possible causes, among others, for his own death two years later. Though he never reaped a rich bounty for his literature during his life, Poe is credited with inventing detective fiction, with spurring others toward science fiction, and with popularizing the short story.

"*Every act should have an aim. We must suffer, we must work, we must pay for our place at the game, but this is for seeing's sake; or at the very least that others may one day see.*"

Poincaré, Henri

Poincaré was one of the great polymaths and scientific thinkers of the nineteenth century; his contributions to modern mathematics and physics are astonishing, and he single-handedly laid the groundwork for many of the discoveries that were made after his death.

Born in Nancy, France, in 1862, Poincaré was an avid reader, and began reading popular science books at a young age before moving to more advanced texts. He had an incredible memory, and preferred linking the ideas he was reading in his head rather than learning by rote memorization. This skill would prove useful when he attended university lectures, as his poor eyesight kept him from being able to see what the professors were writing on the blackboard.

Upon graduation, he became a professor at the University of Paris, where he served for many years. He held positions in multiple departments, including astronomy, physics and mathematics. In 1880 he made the discovery that elliptic and automorphic functions were related to the same set of algebraic equations. He continued to do fundamental work through the 1880s in celestial mechanics and physics.

Poincaré also helped to discover the theory of special relativity with Hendrik Lorentz and Albert Einstein. Einstein would later say that Poincare was one of the pioneers of the theory of relativity. In 1905 Poincare proposed the theory that gravitational waves emanated from bodies with mass, and propagated outward at the speed of light; this was later also predicted by Einstein based on general relativity.

He would go on to work in the field of mining even while he was making breakthrough discoveries in science and mathematics; in 1893 he became a chief engineer in the French Mining Corps, and was promoted to Inspector in 1910. He also worked to coordinate worldwide time in the French Bureau of Longitudes.

Poincaré's contributions to modern science and mathematics were numerous and varied. He contributed to the special theory of relativity and quantum mechanics, Algebraic topology and geometry, electromagnetism, differential equations, to name just a few.

He died on July 12, 1912, at the age of 58 in Paris.

The Three-Body Problem

Predicting the motions of a group of orbiting celestial bodies has been a problem since Sir Isaac Newton first published the *Principia* in 1687. The problem concerns how to correctly predict the individual motions of three or more bodies that are acting on one another gravitationally. Solving the problem would allow physicists to better understand the stability of the Solar System. In 1887 the King of Sweden established a prize for anyone who could solve the problem. Although Poincaré was unable to solve the problem, he was still given the award for his work, which had considerably advanced understanding of celestial mechanics.

The Poincare Conjecture

Poincaré is perhaps most famous for the mathematical conjecture named for him. It proposes that any circle made on its surface can be contracted to a single point: for example, a rubber band wrapped around the sphere can be slid down to a single point. This property is unique in three-dimensional space to the sphere; it is not true for a disk (which has an edge) or a donut-shaped object, for example.

Poincaré's conjecture asks whether the same holds true for a sphere in four-dimensional space. The conjecture directed much of the next century's exploration in mathematics, and in particular the field of topology, which studies the properties of continuous space. The conjecture, proposed in 1904, was not solved until 2003, when Grigori Perelman showed that the same is true for a sphere in four-dimensional space.

More Quotes From Henri Poincaré

"A scientist worthy of the name, above all a mathematician, experiences in his work the same impression as an artist; his pleasure is as great and of the same nature."

"The task of the educator is to make the child's spirit pass again where its forefathers have gone, moving rapidly through certain stages but suppressing none of them. In this regard, the history of science must be our guide."

> *To err is human, to forgive divine.*
>
> *A. Pope.*

Pope, Alexander

An eighteenth-century poet who wrote biting satire, Alexander Pope's quotes remain popular in the English-speaking world.

Alexander Pope was born in London on May 21, 1688, to Catholic parents. Their religion prevented him from being able to attend public school or university, and so Pope mostly educated himself. He learned French, Latin, and Greek on his own, and read the *Odyssey* when he was only six years old. He wrote his first poem, "Ode to Solitude," when he was twelve. That year he also contracted a tuberculosis infection that would deform his spine and stunt his growth.

Pope wrote *Pastorals* when he was sixteen, and they were published in 1710. The *Pastorals* catapulted him to literary fame. The following year he wrote *Essay on Criticism*, a poem in which he first used the heroic couplet that would become his signature style. The *Essay* is the source of many of Pope's most famous quotations. It brought him to the attention of Jonathan Swift and John Gay, who with him formed the Scriblerus Club. The Club included writers who satirized ignorance in the fictional character Martinus Scriblerus, on whom Pope would later base the *Dunciad*.

In 1712 Pope wrote his most famous work, *The Rape of the Lock*. It is an epic poem that tells the story of two wealthy Catholic families who quarrel over a stolen lock of hair. In 1713 he began working on a six-volume translation of the *Iliad*, producing one volume a year. He sold the volumes by subscription, which allowed him to live comfortably on his writing alone. He went on to translate the *Odyssey* and wrote *Essay on Man* in 1734. He died at his estate at Twickenham on May 30, 1744.

More Quotes From Alexander Pope

"For modes of faith let graceless zealots fight; / His can't be wrong whose life is in the right."

"A little Learning is a dang'rous Thing; / Drink deep, or taste not the Pierian Spring: / There shallow Draughts intoxicate the Brain, / And drinking largely sobers us again."

"True ease in writing comes from art, not chance, / As those move easiest who have learn'd to dance."

> *As the greatest things often take their rise from the smallest beginnings, so the worst things sometimes proceed from good intentions.*
>
> —Joseph Priestley

Priestley, Joseph

Joseph Priestley was one of the founders of modern chemistry: he not only discovered oxygen and photosynthesis, but the next time you're enjoying soda water, you can thank him for that, too.

Joseph Priestley was born in 1733 in Yorkshire, England, and was raised by a modest family of cloth-makers. As a Calvinist Dissenter to the Church of England, he was prevented from attending University in England, and instead enrolled in the Dissenters' Academy in Northhamptonshire in 1752. While there, he studied the sciences, philosophy, and literature, and gained a reputation as a stubborn freethinker. He eventually rejected his stern Calvinist upbringing, and co-founded Unitarianism in England.

Early Experiments on Electricity

In 1761 Priestley became a teacher at the Dissenting Academy in Warrington, where he published a number of books on history and philosophy. While there, his interest in science grew, and he began writing a history of the study of electricity. In 1765 Benjamin Franklin visited Warrington, and encouraged Priestley to continue his work on electricity. In the *History and Present State of Electricity*, Priestley's experiments discover that charcoal conducts electricity, describe the inverse square law of electrical attraction, and observe the relationship between electricity and chemical reactions.

He also presented an argument that scientific progress was driven not by the theories proposed by a few men of genius, but rather on discoveries of "new facts" that anyone could make. He roundly rejected dogma and prejudice, arguing for individual inquiry instead. Based on the *History*, Priestley was inducted to the Royal Society of London in 1766.

Investigations in Chemistry and the Discovery of Oxygen

Priestley's discoveries about electricity encouraged him to begin experimenting in the field of chemistry. Over the next twenty years, he published more than a dozen articles describing his experiments on gases and six volumes of his work *Experiments and Observations on Different Kinds of Air*. Prior to his work, chemists had identified three gases: air, fixed air (carbon dioxide), and inflammable air (hydrogen). Priestly discovered ten more: nitric oxide, nitrous oxide, nitrogen dioxide, ammonia, hydrogen chloride, sulfur dioxide, silicon tetrafluoride, carbon monoxide, nitrogen, and, most famously, oxygen.

In August 1774, while in his laboratory, Priestly heated red mercuric oxide, which gave off a colorless gas. He observed that a candle burned at a much greater intensity when it was exposed to the gas. "To complete the proof of the superior quality" of the gas, he placed a mouse in a sealed vessel filled with it. Had the vessel been filled with "common air," he wrote, it would have died within fifteen minutes. Instead, the mouse was still alive and "quite vigorous" an hour later when Priestley removed it from the vessel. Priestly called the gas "dephlogisticated air," based on the belief at the time that phlogiston was an airborne contaminant.

That October Priestley met the French chemist Antoine Lavoisier in Paris, in one of the most important meetings in the history of modern science. Priestley described his experiments to Lavoisier, who not only successfully repeated his experiments, but spent the next five years intensively studying the gas. This would begin a scientific revolution in the field of chemistry that would ultimately overthrow the theory of phlogiston and lead to the advent of modern chemistry.

Exile to America

While still living in England, Priestley's support of the French and American Revolutions was labeled seditious by the government and the press. His home and laboratory were attacked and destroyed by a mob in 1791, and in 1794 he fled to the United States. He died there in 1804, and was buried in Philadelphia.

More Quotes From Joseph Priestley

"In completing one discovery we never fail to get an imperfect knowledge of others of which we could have no idea before, so that we cannot solve one doubt without creating several new ones."

"The mind of man can never be wholly barren. Through our whole lives we are subject to successive impressions; for, either new ideas are continually flowing in, or traces of the old ones are marked deeper."

"The mind of man will never be able to contemplate the being, perfections, and providence of God without meeting with inexplicable difficulties."

"We more easily give our assent to any proposition when the person who contends for it appears, by his manner of delivering himself, to have a perfect knowledge of the subject of it."

> *There are moments when everything goes well; don't be frightened, it won't last.*
>
> —Jules Renard

Renard, Jules

A nineteenth-century French author and member of the Goncourt Literary Society, Jules Renard was acclaimed for his use of irony and cruel circumstances to present comical situations in his writing. His journals provided insight into the life of a Parisian writer in the late nineteenth and early twentieth centuries.

Jules Renard was born on February 22, 1864, in Chalons-du-Maine, France. His father, François Renard, was a laborer who was working on construction of a railroad when he was born. Renard was raised in Nièvre, in central France. His family was of modest means, and Renard's childhood was neither happy nor easy; he would later describe it as "a great ruddy silence." He did not attend formal school, but developed a love of reading at an early age. In 1885 he joined the French military, serving in Bourges for one year.

Work and Legacy

Renard married Marie Morneau in April 1888. The couple moved to Paris that same year and Renard began publishing articles in various Paris newspapers. He wrote prodigiously, publishing short stories, plays, and several novels. He would eventually publish twenty novels between 1888 and 1919, including *Two Fables Without a Moral* in 1893, *The Winemaker in his Vineyard* in 1894, *Les Phillipe* in 1907, and *Ragotte* in 1909. He also wrote seven plays and a posthumously published journal.

Renard's best-known work is *Poil de Carrotte* (*Carrot Head*), published in 1894. *Poil de Carrotte* is a semiautobiographical novel that tells the story of young François Lepic, a redheaded child whose parents are cruel to him. Lepic's father does not care about him one way or the other, and his mother openly hates him. Lepic is subjected to daily humiliations, but uses cunning and wit to maintain his dignity and survive the adult world. The book is notable for its wit and irony, and became a classic of French literature. In 1900 Renard adapted *Poil de Carrotte* into a play with the help of Andre Antoine, a groundbreaking theatre director.

In 1904 Renard was elected mayor of Chitry, his hometown. In 1907 he was inducted into the Goncourt Literary Society, or Academie Goncourt, with the help of his friend Octave Mirbeau. The Goncourt Society was founded in 1903 as an alternative to the French Academy, the preeminent literary society in Paris at the time. The Goncourt Society awards an annual prize for fiction in several categories, and Renard's appointment solidified his status as a literary celebrity in Paris. In 1925 Renard's private journal, which spanned the years 1887 to 1910, was published. It is widely considered a masterwork of introspection and humor, and provides insights into the literary scene in Paris at the turn of the twentieth century.

Renard's work inspired many other writers of the early twentieth century; in particular Somerset Maugham decided to publish his own journals as *The Writer's Notebook* after reading Renard's journals. In the introduction, Maugham praised Renard as the inspiration for the work.

Renard died in on May 22, 1910, in Paris.

More Quotes From Jules Renard

"When the defects of others are perceived with so much clarity, it is because one possesses them oneself."

Understanding is a two-way street.

Eleanor Roosevelt

Roosevelt, Eleanor

As Franklin Delano Roosevelt was the longest-serving president, Eleanor was the longest-serving First Lady. She redefined the position and stayed politically active throughout her lifetime.

Eleanor Roosevelt, born Anna Eleanor Roosevelt, was one of the most influential First Ladies. A niece of Theodore Roosevelt and a distant cousin to Franklin, she grew up in a prominent family, though her parents died when she was young, casting a

shadow over her childhood. Her marriage with Franklin had its difficulties, particularly in its early years. Eleanor struggled with an overbearing mother-in-law, finding out that Franklin had had an affair, and his bout with polio. The couple remained together, however, forging a political partnership. Eleanor urged him to remain politically active after the bout with polio. She herself was active in her husband's campaign for governor of New York, and his later campaigns for the presidency.

As First Lady, Roosevelt gave speeches, wrote columns, and advocated for women and civil rights, becoming a political powerhouse in her own right. At the time, her actions were considered quite controversial. After her husband's death, she remained active, serving as a delegate to the United Nations and later in the Kennedy administration as 1st Chair of the Presidential Commission on the Status of Women. She died in 1962 at the age of 78.

Did She Say It?

Roosevelt is often quoted as the originator of the phrase, "No one can make you feel inferior without your consent." Archivists, however, have not been able to track down a specific occasion on which she said those exact words. It may have been drawn from something Eleanor did say circa 1935 about inferiority, and it was attributed to her as early as 1940 and 1941.

More Quotes From Eleanor Roosevelt

"Will people ever be wise enough to refuse to follow bad leaders or to take away the freedom of other people?"

"One of the best ways of enslaving a people is to keep them from education ... The second way of enslaving a people is to suppress the sources of information, not only by burning books but by controlling all the other ways in which ideas are transmitted."

"Life was meant to be lived, and curiosity must be kept alive. One must never, for whatever reason, turn his back on life."

"You gain strength, courage, and confidence by every experience in which you really stop to look fear in the face. You are able to say to yourself, 'I have lived through this horror. I can take the next thing that comes along.' ... You must do the thing you think you cannot do."

The only thing we have to fear is fear itself.

Roosevelt, Franklin Delano

There's debate as to whether Franklin Delano Roosevelt coined this phrase. Regardless of its origins, though, no one has uttered the words quite the way he did.

The full quote is: "So, first of all, let me assert my firm belief that the only thing we have to fear is fear itself—nameless, unreasoning, unjustified terror which paralyzes needed efforts to convert retreat into advance." Thus said FDR, using his patrician New York diction, in the opening paragraph of his first inaugural address on March 4, 1933.

FDR was certainly a well-educated president, having studied at Groton, Harvard, and Columbia Law School. He was also an eloquent speaker who surrounded himself with talented speechwriters. Still, it appears that Roosevelt appropriated the famous line—and his potential sources include Michel de Montaigne, Francis Bacon, and Henry David Thoreau.

For his part, Roosevelt had good reason to address public fear. The United States floundered in the Great Depression. Russia had gone communist; millions there were dying as the result of famine. In Germany, defeated at great cost fifteen years earlier, Adolf Hitler had his country's young democracy on the ropes.

On the positive side for the United States, it had recently dedicated Mt. Rushmore, and *King Kong* had just hit movie theaters. Small comfort, however, as Roosevelt was preparing Americans for draconian measures. Later in the speech, FDR proclaimed that if necessary he would put matters right with or without the cooperation of Congress, even if he had to seek a formal declaration of war upon "the emergency."

Although he was primarily referring to sweeping economic change, it seems Roosevelt also foresaw war. Most Americans preferred to let the Old World stew in its own tribal conflicts, but FDR saw that this might not be possible—and indeed, it was not.

More Quotes From Franklin Delano Roosevelt

"If I prove a bad president, I will also likely to prove the last president."

"Human kindness has never weakened the stamina or softened the fiber of a free people. A nation does not have to be cruel to be tough."

"The Nation that destroys its soil destroys itself."

"Repetition does not transform a lie into a truth."

> *The only man who makes no mistakes is the man who never does anything.*

Theodore Roosevelt

Roosevelt, Theodore

Theodore Roosevelt viewed the federal government as an arbiter between workers and business owners, protecting the rights of all.

After the assassination of President William McKinley, Theodore Roosevelt became the nation's youngest President just weeks before his forty-third birthday. Frail and sickly as a child of privilege growing up in New York City, he took it upon himself to develop a strong physique and character through what he termed the "strenuous life" of hard work and physical activity.

Roosevelt had a budding political career in New York before the Spanish-American War broke out in 1898. He seized the opportunity to organize a volunteer cavalry known as the Rough Riders, made up of a cross-section of American men that included ranch hands, Ivy League athletes, policemen, and Native American scouts. The cavalry's fame helped him become governor of New York, and vice president soon after.

Upon McKinley's death, Roosevelt took to the presidency with the same energy he applied to all his pursuits. His approach to American industry, balancing the rights of workers with the needs of business owners, initiated the Progressive Era of reform that characterized the next two decades. Speaking at the New York State Fair in 1903, he described his administration's economic policies as a "square deal" that dispensed justice equally to all levels of American production.

The Panama Canal was another major accomplishment of the first years of his administration. The construction of the canal linking the Pacific and Atlantic oceans required not only an enormous feat of engineering but also the wresting of Panama from Colombia. Despite this political interference, the canal was widely viewed as a heroic achievement.

Roosevelt was the first President to be elected to the office after having assumed the title upon the death of his predecessor, and the first President to be awarded the Nobel Peace Prize (for negotiating a treaty ending the Russo-Japanese War). He is also remembered for his conservation efforts protecting the country's natural resources.

More Quotes From Theodore Roosevelt

"We must treat each man on his worth and merits as a man. We must see that each is given a square deal, because he is entitled to no more and should receive no less."

"It is no use to preach to [children] if you do not act decently yourself."

"Let us speak courteously, deal fairly, and keep ourselves armed and ready."

"I don't pity any man who does hard work worth doing. I admire him. I pity the creature who does not work, at whichever end of the social scale he may regard himself as being."

"Death is always and under all circumstances a tragedy, for if it is not, then it means that life itself has become one."

"Greatness means strife for nation and man alike. A soft, easy life is not worth living, if it impairs the fibre of brain and heart and muscle. We must dare to be great; and we must realize that greatness is the fruit of toil and sacrifice and high courage ... "

192192192192192192192 192192192192192 • Rousseau, Jean-Jacques

> *Man is born free; and everywhere he is in chains. One thinks himself the master of others, and still remains a greater slave than they.*

Rousseau, Jean-Jacques

Rousseau's political ideas helped kickstart the Enlightenment, influenced the American and French Revolutions, and reverberate through society to this day.

Jean-Jacques Rousseau was born in Geneva, Switzerland, on June 28, 1712. His mother died when he was an infant, and his father abandoned the child when he was ten years old. He was raised by his aunt and uncle until he left Geneva in 1738. He travelled through Europe for a few years, settling in Paris in 1742. For eleven months in 1743 he served as a secretary to the French ambassador to Venice, and while there he fell in love with Italian opera. But he was often paid late, if at all, and he soon left the post, taking with him a deep mistrust of government and bureaucracy. He returned to Paris, broke and with few job prospects. He fell in love with Therese Levasseur, and they had four children together, but Rousseau coerced her to give them up to an orphanage to newborns as he had no interest in raising them.

In 1750 Rousseau entered an essay competition at the Academie de Dijon. The competition posed the question as to whether the restoration of arts and sciences had contributed to the "purification of morals." Rousseau submitted the essay "Discourse on the Arts and Sciences," which took first place and made him instantly famous. The essay argues that the arts and sciences ultimately ruin human morality. In it, Rousseau first presented the philosophy that he would espouse his entire life: that civilization has a destructive effect on human beings.

The Social Contract

In 1754 Rousseau returned to Geneva, where he joined the Calvinist religion. He wrote the "Discourse on Inequality" in 1755 in response to another competition by the Academie de Dijon. This essay did not win, but in it Rousseau developed the arguments of his 1750 essay. The essay argues that man is essentially good in his natural state, as he existed before

civilization arose, and that society is artificial and corrupt, and that it only results in promoting unhappiness. The essay draws the conclusion that material progress actually destroys any possibility of sincere relationships, and gives rise to jealousy and suspicion. Rousseau further argued that private property is the basis of all inequality.

During the 1750s, Rousseau also wrote novels and composed music. His novel *Julie, ou la nouvelle Heloise*, an epistolary novel that references the letters of Heloise and Abelard, was published in 1761 and was immensely popular. In 1762, he published what would become his most famous philosophical treatise, *The Social Contract*. The book explores the relationship of man to society. Breaking with his earlier writings, in the *Contract* Rousseau argued that the natural state of man is

a brutish one that lacks any morality, and only society can give rise to ethical actors. In nature, he argued, each individual is in constant competition for resources with everyone else. Only by joining with one another to collectively address threats can humans be successful; this arrangement is society, or the social contract.

The Social Contract served as the inspiration for many of the political movements of the second half of the eighteenth century. The work dismisses the divine right of monarchs, arguing that the people are sovereign and have the right to govern themselves. This idea would inspire the American and French Revolutions, and continues to be the dominant political philosophy in Western thought to this day.

Rousseau died on July 2, 1778, at his friend's chateau in Ermenonville, France.

More Quotes From Jean-Jacques Rousseau

"Virtue is a state of war, and to live in it means one always has some battle to wage against oneself."

"An honest man nearly always thinks justly."

"A country cannot subsist well without liberty, nor liberty without virtue."

"Tranquility is found also in dungeons; but is that enough to make them desirable places to live in?"

"What man loses by the social contract is his natural liberty and an unlimited right to everything he tries to get and succeeds in getting; what he gains is civil liberty and the proprietorship of all he possesses."

> *What we think, or what we know, or what we believe is, in the end, of little consequence. The only consequence is what we do.*

Ruskin, John

A leading Victorian art critic, John Ruskin emphasized the connection between nature, art, and society, and is widely considered a forerunner of modern ideas concerning sustainability and the environment.

John Ruskin was born in London on February 8, 1819, to a merchant family; his father had made a fortune in the wine trade. Ruskin was an only child and homeschooled; his father's extensive collection of watercolor paintings influenced him at an early age. He also travelled extensively as a child with his family, which further developed his ideas on nature and society. He attended Oxford for five years, where he won the Newdigate Prize for his poetry. He also worked for much of his time at Oxford on an extensive, though unfinished, dissertation on the painter JMW Turner, a Romanticist landscape painter.

Art Criticism

He began publishing short essays on art criticism in the 1830s, and in 1843 he published the first of what would become the five-volume series *Modern Painters*. The work drew on Ruskin's amateur fascination with botany and geology, and the first volume dealt extensively with the themes of Nature in Turner's paintings, defending what he considered the "truths" of his work, examining tone, color, space, earth, water, and vegetation in turn. Ruskin would continue working on *Modern Painters* until the fifth volume was published in 1860.

Ruskin wrote his art criticism in a plain style of prose that both vividly described the works he was discussing and made his writing accessible to a wide audience. In doing so, he introduced the possibility of art appreciation to a many newly wealthy members of the commercial and professional classes.

He urged young painters to seek the meanings of art in Nature, "rejecting nothing, selecting nothing, and scorning nothing."

Following the publication of the first volume of *Modern Painters*, Ruskin turned his attention to architecture; in 1849, following his honeymoon with Effie Gray touring Gothic churches in northern France, he wrote *The Seven Lamps of Architecture*, in which he argued for seven moral principles that should guide architecture. His respect for original style in architecture would inspire the architecture conservation movement of the twentieth century. In 1851 he published the first volume of *The Stones of Venice*. The book is primarily a history of the architecture of that city, but it also argues that art and architecture are the manifestation of the social conditions that produce them. He said, "All great art is the work of the whole living creature, body, and soul, and chiefly of the soul."

In 1851 his marriage fell apart, and Ruskin began travelling extensively. He published more volumes of *Modern Painters* and *The Stones of Venice*, and in 1858 he began teaching painting to the daughters of Maria La Touche. He became infatuated with Rose La Touche, who was a child at the time, and when she turned eighteen he asked her to marry him. She put him off for three years, until she finally refused in 1872. She died following a long illness in 1875, and Ruskin fell into a deep depression marked by severe breakdowns.

Ruskin was appointed a Professor of Fine Art at Oxford in 1870, and while there he wrote and published *Fors Clavigera*, a monthly magazine of cultural theory. While there, he published *Fiction Fair & Foul*, a discussion of English writers, and *The Storm-Cloud of the Nineteenth Century*, which studied the effects of industrial pollution on weather patterns. Between

1885 and 1889 he wrote *Praeterita*, his autobiography, but never finished it. He died on January 20, 1900.

More Quotes From John Ruskin

"You may either win your peace, or buy it:—win it, by resistance to evil;—buy it, by compromise with evil."

"Let us reform our schools, and we shall find little reform needed in our prisons."

"That country is the richest which nourishes the greatest number of noble and happy human beings."

"Give a little love to a child, and you get a great deal back."

"When men are rightly occupied, their amusement grows out of their work ... But now, having no true business, we pour our whole masculine energy into the false business of money-making; and having no true emotion, we must have false emotions dressed up for us to play with, not innocently, as children with dolls, but guiltily and darkly."

"A little group of wise hearts is better than a wilderness full of fools."

> *Yesterday is done.
> Tomorrow never comes.
> Today is here. If you
> don't know what to do,
> sit still and listen.*
> —Carl Sandburg

Sandburg, Carl

Carl Sandburg hailed from Galesburg, Illinois, the son of Swedish immigrants to the United States. The family struggled, so Carl left school in his early teen-age years to lay bricks, wash dishes, and tackle several other odd jobs to bring in a few extra dimes. At seventeen, he hit the road for Kansas with little more than the clothes on his back. When life as a hobo wore on him, he enlisted and spent eight months in Puerto Rico during the Spanish-American War.

Sandburg, though, was neither a soldier nor a brick-layer. He was a writer—a revelation that would come out after he worked to put himself through Lombard College just after the turn of the century. He left in 1903 without a degree, but the encouragement he received there to pursue his writing inspired him to give it a go.

He published a pamphlet called "Reckless Ecstasy" in 1904. He then took a job as a newspaper and advertising writer in Milwaukee, where he met his wife, Lillian (Paula) Steichen. He assisted Milwaukee's first Socialist mayor from 1910–12. And it was a move to Chicago to write for the *Daily News* that truly turned his career.

A member of Chicago's literary renaissance along with Ben Hecht, Theodore Dreiser, Sherwood Anderson, and Edgar Lee Master, Sandburg reached the masses writing about the city and its industry. His *Chicago Poems* of 1916 included "Chicago," which gave the town its "big shoulders" nickname.

Two years later, his *Cornhuskers* collection led to a Pulitzer Prize. More than three decades later, he added a second Pulitzer for his *Complete Poems* (1950).

Sandburg wrote for children and adults, he wrote plenty about President Abraham Lincoln, and he never lost the passion for capturing life in the Midwest right up until his death at eighty-nine in 1967.

More Quotes From Carl Sandburg

"There are some people who can receive a truth by no other way than to have their understanding shocked and insulted."

"Back of every mistaken venture and defeat is the laughter of wisdom, if you listen."

"I'm an idealist. I don't know where I'm going, but I'm on my way."

"I am the people—the mob—the crowd—the mass. / Do you know that all the great work of the world is done through me?"

"Poetry is the opening and closing of a door, leaving those who look through to guess about what is seen during a moment."

"Time is the coin of your life. You spend it. Do not allow others to spend it for you."

> " *Those who cannot remember the past are condemned to repeat it.* "
>
> —George Santayana

Santayana, George

George Santayana was a Spanish-American cultural critic and philosopher who coined many popular aphorisms and originated the definition of beauty as "pleasure objectified."

Jorge Agustín Nicolás Ruiz de Santayana y Borrás was born in Madrid on December 16, 1863. When he was nine, his family moved to Boston, where he attended the Boston Latin School. Santayana graduated from Harvard in 1886, and spent two years studying philosophy at the University of Berlin. In 1889 he received a Ph.D. in philosophy and began teaching philosophy at Harvard. Santayana's students included luminaries such as T.S. Eliot, Robert Frost, Gertrude Stein, and

W.E.B. Du Bois. He published *The Sense of Beauty*, a study of aesthetics, in 1896. This was the first major work on aesthetics writing in the United States. Santayana was later reported to have said he only wrote the book because he was under pressure to publish to be granted tenure.

He wrote his five-volume *The Life of Reason* in 1905–06. It is considered the first major work on the philosophy of Pragmatism and is the source of the quote above. He was made a full professor at Harvard in 1907, but following the death of his mother in 1912, he resigned his position and remained in Europe for the rest of his life, settling permanently in Rome in 1924. He wrote *The Realms of Being* from 1927–1942. The four-volume work deals with truth, materialism, and human consciousness. An atheist, he described himself as an "aesthetic Catholic," and had an affinity for the culture of the Roman church.

Santayana died on September 26, 1952.

More Quotes From George Santayana

"There is no cure for birth and death save to enjoy the interval."

"Matters of religion should never be matters of controversy. We neither argue with a lover about his taste, nor condemn him, if we are just, for knowing so human a passion."

"It is not society's fault that most men seem to miss their vocation. Most men have no vocation."

"Progress, far from consisting in change, depends on retentiveness. When change is absolute there remains no being to improve and no direction is set for possible improvement: and when experience is not retained, as among savages, infancy is perpetual. Those who cannot remember the past are condemned to repeat it."

"Fanaticism consists in redoubling your efforts when you have forgotten your aim."

"That life is worth living is the most necessary of assumptions and, were it not assumed, the most impossible of conclusions."

"Happiness is the only sanction of life; where happiness fails, existence remains a mad and lamentable experiment."

"Beauty as we feel it is something indescribable: what it is or what it means can never be said."

Mostly it is loss which teaches us about the worth of things.

Arthur Schopenhauer

Schopenhauer, Arthur

Arthur Schopenhauer was born on February 22, 1788, in Danzig (present-day Gdańsk). His father Heinrich was a wealthy merchant, and his mother would become a famous writer. In 1793 Danzig was annexed by the Kingdom of Prussia, and the family moved to Hamburg. Schopenhauer was given an excellent education. When his father died in 1805, he had to work for two years as a merchant; his mother and sister moved to Weimar, where his mother opened a literary *salon* and befriended other writers such as Goethe and Christoph Wieland. In 1809 Schopenhauer was able to finally attend the University of Göttingen, where he studied the natural sciences before switching to the humanities. He immersed himself in the works of Plato and Immanuel Kant. In 1811 Schopenhauer began attending the Univerity of Berlin, and earned a doctorate in philosophy from the University of Jena in 1813.

Schopenhauer spent the winter of 1814 in Weimar, where he met Goethe at his mother's *salon*. A historian named Friedrich Majer introduced Schopenhauer to the Hindu *Vedas* and *Upanishads*. This was a pivotal moment in Schopenhauer's philosophical development. He would later cite the *Vedas*, along with Plato and Kant's writings, as the foundation upon which he built his own philosophical ideas. In spite of a strained relationship with his mother, her status as a best-selling novelist allowed Schopenhauer access to her publishing house, and helped him get several of his early works published. The following spring, he left Weimar and moved to Dresden, where he wrote *On Vision and Colors* in 1816 in support of Goethe's 1810 treatise *The Theory of Colors*.

The World as Will and Representation

In 1814 Schopenhauer had begun working on what would become his masterwork: *The World as Will and Representation*, published in 1819. The work consists of four volumes that comprehensively address the theory of knowledge and develop a philosophy of the natural world. Schopenhauer rejected the philosophy of Immanuel Kant, asserting that the world as we understand it is only a representation of the real world and not the world in its true essence. One can know themselves in two ways: externally, or as they appear, and internally, as part of what Schopenhauer saw as the essence of all things in the universe, and referred to as the Will, or, very simply, the will to live.

The Will, he argues, is the essence of everything, and exists independently of space and time, of purpose and causation. It manifests beginning in the inorganic reactions in nature, through living organisms in nature, and ultimately to humanity's rational actions. At the end of this ascension is only death, the apex of the Will. Schopenhauer argued that the ascension of the Will is fraught with misery and suffering, and only by denying it can one transcend suffering. The first two books deal extensively with this philosophy; the second two and discussed the meaning of aesthetics and ethics. Schopenhauer contended that all ethics are based on two impulses: the affirmation or denial of the Will.

Schopenhauer's work did not receive a great deal of attention when it was published, but it would be hugely significant, and influenced the work of Freud, Nietzsche, Tolstoy, Jung, and Camus, among many others. After lecturing briefly at the University of Berlin beginning in 1820, he retired to Frankfurt in 1833, where he would remain for the next twenty-eight years. He died on September 21, 1860.

More Quotes From Arthur Schopenhauer

"We forfeit three-fourths of ourselves in order to be like other people."

"The bad thing about all religions is that, instead of being able to confess their allegorical nature, they have to conceal it … "

"Change alone is eternal, perpetual, immortal."

"The effect of music is so very much more powerful and penetrating than is that of the other arts, for these others speak only of the shadow, but music of the essence."

"Talent hits a target no one else can hit; Genius hits a target no one else can see."

"Life is a business that does not cover the costs."

> *Things that were hard to bear are sweet to remember.*
> —Seneca the Younger

Seneca, Lucius Annaeus

Seneca the Younger was Nero's closest advisor—but he would be accused of treachery and forced to commit suicide by Nero himself.

Seneca the Younger was born Lucius Annaeus Seneca in Cordoba in 4 BCE and raised in Rome. His father was Seneca the Elder, a wealthy Roman equestrian and writer. Not much is known about Seneca's life until he became the advisor to the Emperor Nero in 54 CE. In the first few years in this role, Seneca, along with another advisor, Sextus Burrus, was

able to heavily influence Nero and his rule. But they soon lost their sway over him. In 59, when Nero ordered the murder of his mother Agrippina during a power struggle, they went along with the plot.

Seneca wrote twelve essays on Stoic philosophy and morality that advocated living simply and in accordance with nature. His essays encourage the reader to accept suffering and death as normal parts of life. He also wrote at least ten tragedies; those that survived heavily influenced English theatre, including Shakespheare's tragedies *Hamlet* and *Titus Andronicus*.

According to the historian Dio, Seneca's actions were often at odds with his writing. Dio considered Seneca to be a hypocrite of the worst kind; one who railed against tyranny "while making himself the teacher of a tyrant."

Seneca retired to his country estate in 62 after the death of Burrus. In 65, however, he was implicated in a plot to murder Nero. The Senate was growing unhappy with Nero's increasingly dictatorial leadership, and convinced Gaius Piso, a leading statesman, to lead a plot to seize power. The plot was uncovered and Nero ordered the conspirators, including Seneca, to commit suicide.

More Quotes From Seneca the Younger

"What fools these mortals be."

"Once again prosperous and successful crime goes by the name of virtue; good men obey the bad, might is right and fear oppresses law."

"Of war men ask the outcome, not the cause."

"Authority founded on injustice is never of long duration."

"Who profits by a sin has done the sin."

"It is not the man who has too little, but the man who craves more, that is poor."

"For love of bustle is not industry—it is only the restlessness of a hunted mind."

"Live among men as if God beheld you; speak to God as if men were listening."

"If one doesn't know his mistakes, he won't want to correct them."

"That most knowing of persons—gossip."

"It is better, of course, to know useless things than to know nothing."

"Friendship is always helpful, but love sometimes even does harm."

> *Ideals are like stars; you will not succeed in touching them with your hands. But like the seafaring man on the desert of waters, you choose them as your guides, and following them you will reach your destiny.*

C. Schurz

Shurz, Carl

A German-American revolutionary, politician, journalist, and social reformer, Carl Shurz was the first German immigrant elected to the U.S. Senate, where he fought for higher moral standards in government.

Carl Schurz was born on March 2, 1829, near Cologne, in what was then Prussia. He attended school for only a few years, as his family was too poor to pay for his education, and he was forced to drop out before he graduated. Later, he was able to pass an equivalence examination that allowed him to enroll in the University of Bonn. While he was there he became involved in the German Nationalist revolution of 1848, publishing a nationalist newspaper with his friend Gottfried Kinkel. In 1849 he joined the armed struggle for German independence and fought in a number of battles against the Prussian Army as an artillery officer. When the German forces were defeated at the siege of Rastatt later that year, Schurz was able to escape, making his way to Zürich. He returned to Prussia in 1850, where he helped Kinkel escape from prison. The pair made their way to Great Britain, where Schurz made a living as a German teacher. He married Margarethe Meyer in 1852, and together they immigrated to America. Margarethe would later establish the kindergarten system in the United States.

The couple arrived in Philadelphia in July, but eventually settled in Wisconsin, where Schurz almost immediately became involved in local politics. He joined the Republican Party and began doing anti-slavery organizing. In 1857 he ran unsuccessfully for Lieutenant Governor, and in 1858 he volunteered for Abraham Lincoln's Senate campaign.

The Civil War

Schurz was commissioned as a brigadier general in the Union Army and took command of a division in 1862. In August of 1862 he led troops at the Second Battle of Bull Run. He was promoted to major general and the following year he led the Union Army's Ninth Corps he fought at Chancellorsville, Gettysburg, and Chattanooga. His Ninth Corps was routed by Stonewall Jackson's troops at Chancellorsville, and they again retreated at the battle of Gettysburg, leading the press to criticize German-American units in the Union Army. In the final months of the war, Schurz served with General Sherman's Army during the March to the Sea.

Following the war, he toured the Southern states on behalf of President Andrew Johnson. Schurz was a staunch advocate for the rights of African-Americans, and he delivered a report to the President that recommended allowing Southern states to rejoin the Union with full rights. Johnson disagreed, and ignored his report.

Schurz and his wife moved to Detroit in 1866, where he became the editor of the *Detroit Post*. In 1867 they moved again, to St. Louis, where he became editor of the *St. Louis Westliche Post*. While in Missouri, he had his first and only electoral victory in 1869, and served as a U.S. Senator until 1875. He fought political corruption and opposed federal troops enforcing Reconstruction-era laws or extending full rights to African-Americans. In 1872, breaking with President Ulysses S. Grant on these and other issues, he founded the Liberal Republican Party, which opposed a second term for the President. He returned to the Party to support Rutherford B. Hayes, and was granted an appointment as Secretary of the Interior, where he served from 1877–1881.

Following his career in public service, Schurz returned to journalism, editing the *New York Evening Post* and *The Nation*. He died on May 14, 1906, in New York City.

> *Anyone who holds a true opinion without understanding is like a blind man on the right road.*
> —Socrates

Socrates

Socrates was born in Athens circa 470 BCE. We know about him largely through the writings of his students, including Plato and Xenophon. His method of testing philosophical ideas—the Socratic Method—laid the foundation for Western philosophy and logic.

Socrates was born in Athens circa 470 BCE. It's thought that he worked as a mason before devoting himself to philosophy, and he also briefly served in the Athenian army. He had three sons with his wife Xanthippe, but was not much of a family man, preferring to devote himself to educating Athens' youth.

Socrates taught that philosophy should advance the greater wellbeing of society. He was perhaps the first philosopher to propose a system of ethics based on human reason instead of theological dogma. Because human choices are motivated by the desire to be happy, and because wisdom is couched in knowing oneself, he argued, the more a person knows the better they will be able to reason and make choices that bring true happiness. Socrates thought that this logically meant government worked best when it was ruled by knowledgeable, virtuous, and completely self-aware individuals, or what he called philosopher kings.

Socrates strolled the streets of Athens, asking questions of nobles and commoners alike in an effort to find

truths, rather than lecture about what he did know. The Socratic Method of questioning fellow Athenians was designed to force them to think through a problem and realize the conclusion themselves.

Trial and Execution

Athens was undergoing a period of political turmoil during his life, and Socrates publicly attacked what he considered the backwards thinking. As a result, he was arrested and tried for heresy and "corrupting the minds" of Athenian youth. Found guilty, he was sentenced to death by drinking a mixture containing poison hemlock in 399 BCE.

More Quotes From Socrates

"I only wish that wisdom were the kind of thing that flowed ... from the vessel that was full to the one that was empty."
—quoted by Plato

"Wonder is the feeling of a philosopher, and philosophy begins in wonder."
—quoted by Theaetetus

"I myself know nothing, except just a little, enough to extract an argument from another man who is wise and to receive it fairly."
—quoted by Theaetetus

"I am not an Athenian or a Greek, but a citizen of the world."
—quoted by Plutarch

"Bad men live that they may eat and drink, whereas good men eat and drink that they may live."
—quoted by Plutarch

> ## The greatest griefs are those we cause ourselves.
>
> —Sophocles

Sophocles

Born in Attica in 496 BCE, Sophocles was one of the greatest playwrights of ancient Greece, and one of only three whose works have survived to this day. He wrote dozens of plays in his life, but only seven remain in complete form: *Ajax, Antigone, The Women of Trachis, Oedipus the King, Electra, Phioctetes*, and *Oedipus at Colonus*.

Sophocles was the son of a wealthy merchant, and was given a traditional aristocratic education, where he studied the arts. At the age of sixteen, he was selected to lead a boys' choir at a festival held to celebrate a military victory over the Persians. In 468 BCE he defeated the preeminent poet Aeschylus in a competitive recitation, solidifying his reputation as a great writer. In 441 BCE Euripides defeated Sophocles in the annual Athenian dramatic competition. Beginning with his first victory, however, Sophocles won the competition as many as twenty times.

He wrote approximately 120 plays during his lifetime. Sophocles was the first playwright to add a third actor to a play, which was a major development in dramatic theatre. Prior to his work the chorus played a larger role in plot exposition. Sophocles also didn't present his tragedies in trilogy format, which allowed him to pack all of the action into a single play, affording the possibility to heighten the drama. He led a transformation of Greek tragedy from focusing on religion and morality to highlighting the fates and tribulations of individuals.

Some of his most famous characters are Oedipus, the mythical Greek king of Thebes; Antigone who defied a royal decree and put the will of the gods first; and Ajax, a warrior who fought in the Trojan War.

Sophocles died in 406 BCE in Athens.

More Quotes From Sophocles

"Nobly to live, or else nobly to die, befits proud birth."

"Kindness begs kindness evermore."

"Men of ill judgment oft ignore the good that lies within their hands, till they have lost it."

"*What dreadful knowledge of the truth can be when there's no help in truth!*"

"*The greatest griefs are those we cause ourselves.*"

"*Time eases all things.*"

"*I have nothing but contempt for the kind of governor who is afraid, for whatever reason, to follow the course he knows is best for the State.*"

"*Nobody likes the man who brings bad news.*"

"*Grief teaches the steadiest minds to waver.*"

"*Wisdom outweighs any wealth.*"

"*One word frees us of all the weight and pain of life: That word is love.*"

> *[W]e must take care not to admit as true anything, which is only probable. For when one falsity has been let in, infinite others follow.*
>
> —Baruch Spinoza

Spinoza, Baruch

Baruch Spinoza was one of the most important Western philosophers of the seventeenth century. He contributed to numerous areas of philosophy, and he combined influences from numerous historical figures and great philosophers from classical antiquity and his contemporaries.

Baruch Spinoza was born in Amsterdam on November 24, 1632. His family was of Sephardic Jewish descent, having settled in Amsterdam after fleeing the Portuguese Inquisition of 1536. In addition to speaking Portuguese at home, Spinoza learned Dutch, Spanish, Hebrew, and Latin. He attended a Torah yeshiva as a child, and when he was seventeen he began working for his father's import business. Three years later he began studying Latin with Franciscus Enden. Enden introduced the young man to modern philosophy and progressive political and scientific ideas, including the works of Descartes. In his mid-twenties he grew disillusioned with Judaism, and when he made his ideas known, he was excommunicated by the congregation of his Temple. He spent the rest of his life developing his philosophy.

Spinoza's best known work is his treatise *Ethics*, which he wrote in 1664–65 and published in 1667. In it he argued for an ethics that grows out of a system of metaphysics that identifies God with Nature. Rather than being the removed creator and ruler of the universe, Spinoza argued that God was Nature itself, and that Nature is an infinite and deterministic system. He wrote that humans could only find happiness by seeking a rational understanding of the Natural system.

Spinoza's ideas were controversial for his time. In 1670 he moved to The Hague, where he worked on scientific essays and a political treatise. On February 20, 1677, he died at his home in The Hague.

More Quotes From Baruch Spinoza

"Nature abhors a vacuum."

"Beauty, my dear Sir, is not so much a quality of the object beheld, as an effect in him who beholds it. If our sight were longer or shorter, or if our constitution were different, what now appears beautiful to us would seem misshapen, and what we now think misshapen we should regard as beautiful."

"Nature is satisfied with little; and if she is, I am also."

"A free man thinks of death least of all things; and his wisdom is a meditation not of death but of life."

"Nature offers nothing that can be called this man's rather than another's; but, under nature, everything belongs to all— that is, they have authority to claim it for themselves."

"I make this chief distinction between religion and superstition, that the latter is founded on ignorance, the former on knowledge ... "

"Truth is a standard both of itself and of falsity."

> *Come, come, my conservative friend, wipe the dew off your spectacles, and see that the world is moving.*

Elizabeth Cady Stanton

Stanton, Elizabeth Cady

Elizabeth Cady Stanton was one of the founders of the women's rights movement. She called for the Seneca Falls Convention on women's rights, helped write the Convention's Declaration of Sentiments, and advocated for the vote as president of the National Woman Suffrage Association.

Elizabeth Cady was born in Johnstown, New York, on November 12, 1815. She attended Emma Willard's Troy Female Seminary, graduating in 1832. She often visited the home of her cousin Gerrit Smith, a social reformer and abolitionist, and their discussions shaped her early ideas about abolition, temperance, and equal rights for women. In 1840 Cady married

Henry Stanton, himself a social reformer. She kept her own last name, and the couple removed the word "obey" from their marriage vows. On their honeymoon, they travelled to London to attend the World's Anti-Slavery Convention.

Seneca Falls and the Women's Rights Movement

At the Convention, the men in attendance voted to exclude the women from participating, and forced them to sit in a segregated section. Cady Stanton, along with other women in attendance, was outraged. She met with Lucretia Mott, and there the two discussed holding a worldwide convention on women's rights for the first time. Cady Stanton and Mott would remain friends and collaborators for the rest of their lives.

In 1848 their vision of a women's rights convention became reality at Seneca Falls, New York. At the convention, Cady Stanton pushed for the adoption of a resolution that declared obtaining suffrage for women was a key tenet of the women's rights movement. There was initial opposition to the resolution. Nevertheless she persisted, and with the support of Frederick Douglass and other attendees, it passed; "Resolved, That it is the duty of the women of this country to secure to themselves their sacred right to the elective franchise. She also helped draft the Declaration of Sentiments that laid out the goals of the movement.

Cady Stanton worked on the cause of abolishing slavery during the Civil War, and afterwards she continued to work for women's rights. In 1868 she began publishing the weekly newspaper *Revolution* with Susan B. Anthony, and co-founded the National Woman Suffrage Association (NWSA) with Anthony in 1869. She became the organization's first president, and held the post for the next twenty years, when the NWSA merged with the American Woman Suffrage Association. Cady Stanton served as president of the joint organization, the National American Woman Suffrage Association, for two years.

Later Life and Work

Cady Stanton travelled regularly as a speaker on women's rights, including issues that went beyond suffrage: she advocated reforms of women's custody rights, birth control access, property and employment rights, and the right to divorce. She strongly advocated for a woman's right to ride a bicycle, and promoted the concept of the New Woman, who was independent and mobile. She opposed the Fourteenth and Fifteenth Amendments on the grounds that they did not include women. This led to a major break in the women's rights movement between those suffragists who supported extending the vote to African-American men first and women second, and those who advocated universal suffrage. She called for an amendment that would extend the vote to women, first at Seneca Falls and for the remainder of her life.

Between 1881 and 1886, she worked with Anthony and Matilda Joslyn Gage on the first three volumes of the *History of Woman Suffrage*, and in 1895 she published the first volume of *The Woman's Bible*. Cady Stanton had long held that organized religion helped to prevent women from obtaining equal rights. The second volume was published in 1898.

Elizabeth Cady Stanton died on October 26, 1902. Eighteen years later, on August 18, 1920, the Nineteenth Amendment was passed, guaranteeing women the right to vote.

> *The truth is the kindest thing we can give folks in the end.*
>
> *H B Stowe*

Stowe, Harriet Beecher

Harriet Beecher Stowe, a first-time novelist from Cincinnati, dramatized the problem of slavery for all to see in *Uncle Tom's Cabin*.

When Harriet Beecher Stowe was introduced to President Abraham Lincoln, as the story goes, he said, "So, you're the little woman who wrote the book that started this great war." There's no question that few elements fueled the flames of hate across the country as much as *Uncle Tom's Cabin* did. Stowe's story of Tom, a saintly black slave, and the difficult life he and his fellow slaves endured, earned either praise or condemnation. Abolitionists across the North thought it was brilliant and oh-so-true. Southern critics, however, complained that it was completely inaccurate in how it portrayed plantation life.

Borrowing from Real Life

Stowe was a dedicated abolitionist who was more concerned about illustrating the evils of slavery than creating an accurate view of life on the plantation. Although she lived in Cincinnati for eighteen years, just across the river from the slave state of Kentucky, she had little actual experience with Southern plantations. The information in most of her book was taken either from abolitionist literature or her own imagination. Stowe was researching a series of articles she intended to write when she heard about a slave woman who escaped from her masters in Kentucky across the frozen Ohio River. She immediately realized that she could use such a scene in a book. One of the most exciting parts of *Uncle Tom's Cabin* features Eliza, the slave heroine, escaping across the ice.

A Publishing Sensation

Uncle Tom's Cabin first appeared in 1851, serialized in the abolitionist newspaper *National Era*. Its popularity there led to the book's publication as a complete work the next year. It was an instant success, selling 10,000 copies in the first week and more than 300,000 by the end of its first year. *Uncle Tom's Cabin* had even greater popularity in Britain, where more than one million copies sold within a year. Stowe exposed the general public to an issue that most knew very little about. But the book didn't simply educate its readers—it also provoked heated debates in state and federal legislatures.

Interestingly, given today's negative meaning of the term "Uncle Tom," the character in Stowe's book demonstrated strength and traits that were quite heroic. In one instance, when ordered to whip a sickly female slave, Tom refuses and suffers the lash himself. He is ultimately killed by his wicked master, Simon Legree, because he will not betray two runaway slaves. When Legree tries to have the information beaten out of him, Tom goes to his death without revealing a thing.

Not Controversial Enough?

As shocking as some found *Uncle Tom's Cabin*, many— particularly radical abolitionists—didn't think the book went far enough in denouncing slavery. Others, usually those who lived in the South, condemned the book as grossly exaggerated. One of Stowe's admirers was William Lloyd Garrison, the editor of abolitionist newspaper *The Liberator*. "I estimate the value of antislavery writing by the abuse it brings," he wrote to tell her. "Now all the defenders of slavery have let me alone and are abusing you."

More Quotes From Harriet Beecher Stowe

"That ignorant confidence in one's self and one's future, which comes in life's first dawn, has a sort of mournful charm in experienced eyes, who know how much it all amounts to."

"In the old times, women did not get their lives written, though I don't doubt many of them were much better worth writing than the men's."

"Any mind that is capable of a real sorrow is capable of good."

> *[W]hile we are cowards before petty troubles, great sorrows make us brave by rousing our truer [humanity].*

Tagore, Rabindranath

Rabindranath Tagore was an Indian poet and musician who had a major impact on Indian art and literature in the nineteenth century. In 1913 he became the first non-European person to be awarded a Nobel Prize for Literature.

Rabindranath Tagore was born May 7, 1861, the youngest son of Debendranath Tagore. His father was the leader of the Brahmo Samaj, a Hindu sect in nineteenth-century in Bengal, in northeast India. The sect was focused on reviving what it saw as the fundamentals of Hinduism as they were described in the *Upanishads*. Tagore was educated at home by his father, and when he was seventeen years old he was sent to England to receive a formal education, although he did not complete his studies there.

When he returned to India, he managed the family estates. This experience brought him into close contact with many of the laborers who were employed by his family, and this led to him becoming interested in social reforms. He founded a school at Shantiniketan where he attempted to incorporate the ideals of Brahmo Samaj into the educational program. For a number of years, Tagore was active in the Indian Home Rule movement, and was close friends with Mahatma Gandhi.

Literary Success

Tagore had begun writing poetry when he was only eight years old, and released his first collection of poetry when he was sixteen. The collection, which he released under the pseudonym *Bhānusimha*, was initially thought to be long-lost poetry from antiquity. In the 1870s he began publishing short stories under his own name, and he quickly enjoyed critical success. He became known in the West when his poems were translated into English, and he soon began traveling through Europe on lecture circuits. As his fame grew in the beginning of the twentieth century, Tagore met with many other luminaries of the day, including Albert Einstein, Ezra Pound, William Butler Yeats, and George Bernard Shaw. He toured South America, the United States, Asia and the Soviet Union.

Tagore had a very significant impact on the Bengal Renaissance, writing hundreds of poems in over fifty volumes, eight novels, more than eighty short stories, and composing more than two thousand songs. He also was a prolific artist, and made dozens of drawings and paintings. In 1913, he became the first non-European to receive the Nobel Prize for Literature for his collection *Gitanjali: Song Offerings*, published the previous year.

Political Views

Tagore was opposed to imperialism, and supported Indian independence. He worked with Gandhi to promote the cause, and discussed his political views in *Manast*, which he wrote when he was still in his twenties. In 1915 King George V bestowed a knighthood on Tagore. In 1919, following the Jallianwala Bagh massacre, in which British troops killed as many as a thousand unarmed civilians, Tagore renounced his knighthood in protest. He preferred to promote education as the remedy to British colonialism rather than support all-out revolution. This view drew the ire of many Indian nationalists, and he was nearly assassinated during a trip to San Francisco in 1916. He wrote several popular nationalist songs in support of independence.

Tagore continued writing until his final days. He wrote short stories in 1940 and 1941, as well as poetry that is considered some of his finest work, in spite of the fact that his health was failing and he was suffering from chronic pain. He died at home on August 7, 1941.

More Quotes From Rabindranath Tagore

"The truth comes as conqueror only because we have lost the art of receiving it as guest."

"In this playhouse of infinite forms I have had my play, and here have I caught sight of him that is formless."

"The idea of the Nation is one of the most powerful anaesthetics that Man has invented. Under the influence of its fumes the whole people can carry out its systematic programme of the most virulent self-seeking without being in the least aware of its moral perversion, in fact feeling dangerously resentful if it is pointed out."

"There is only one history—the history of Man. All national histories are merely chapters in the larger one."

"When old words die out on the tongue, new melodies break forth from the heart; and where the old tracks are lost, new country is revealed with its wonders."

"The human soul is on its journey from the law to love, from discipline to liberation, from the moral plane to the spiritual."

> *So live your life that the fear of death can never enter your heart. Trouble no one about their religion; respect others in their view, and demand that they respect yours. Love your life, perfect your life, beautify all things in your life.*
>
> —Tecumseh

Tecumseh

Tecumseh became a legend not only for his brave leadership in battle, but for the words he shared with a nation in turmoil. The Shawnee chief inspired his people and fought many brave battles before being killed in the Battle of the Thames in 1813.

Tecumseh was born in Ohio in 1768. His father, Puckshinwau, was a Shawnee war chief, though Tecumseh would far surpass him in battle and political influence. He was just six when his father was killed in the French and Indian War, and the son was not far from carrying on the family tradition. Tecumseh stood out as a warrior, even as a teenager. He joined the American Indian Confederacy under Mohawk chief Joseph Brant, and learned that a union of tribes was best suited to thwarting encroachment on their territories, a stance he would rally behind as he became a chief himself.

His mother took the family to Missouri after the death of his father, and Tecumseh and his older brother Chiksika participated in a series of successful raids against settlements in Kentucky and Tennessee. By 1800 Tecumseh was a prominent Shawnee chief and a leader among his people. His bravery and keen intellect made him well-equipped to head up the efforts to fight those who were looking to slaughter Native Americans.

He envisioned a confederacy of tribes, united in their efforts to protect their people and their lands. When other tribal chiefs signed treaties giving up their land to white frontiersman, Tecumseh argued that they should have their thumbs cut off.

Fighting for Their Lives

Tecumseh and his people were fighting for their lives, quite literally, in the early 1800s. One of his younger brothers, Lalawethica, experienced a series of visions that promised a land of religious deliverance for Native Americans, changed his name to Tenskwatawa and began preaching the good news to his people. Tecumseh was reluctant to believe until the summer of 1806, when his brother correctly predicted a solar eclipse. With that, the chief was swayed.

There was still the matter of preserving their lives and land, however. Tecumseh and his brother moved their settlement to present-day Indiana in 1808, to the confluence of the Tippecanoe and Wabash rivers. Tecumseh stepped up his efforts to unite tribes as one confederacy against the invading white man. They traveled throughout the Midwest, preaching the absurdity of selling or signing away Indian land—land that the "Great Spirit" had given to their people. He was only partially successful.

While several tribes of Native Americans did have degrees of success defending themselves and their land against invaders, bad news was on the horizon. Tecumseh was on a southern trip, trying to recruit the Creeks to join him, when American forces marched against his settlement in November of 1811, burning residences and depleting the food supply.

The War of 1812 followed. Tecumseh went north, to Michigan, and fought valiantly in helping British troops capture Detroit. At one point, Tecumseh led a group of 400 men who charged out of the woods, then circled back around and did it again to make it appear as though there were twice as many forces under his lead. The maneuver worked, prompting the opposing general to surrender.

However, Tecumseh was killed at the Battle of the Thames in 1813. He remains a revered figure in Native American lore for his bravery, intellect, oratory skills and desire to bring unity among the tribes.

> *Moderation in all things. (Not anything in excess).*
>
> —Terence

Terence

Born in Carthage, North Africa, in either 195 or 185 BCE, Terence was taken to Rome as the slave of the Roman Senator Terentius Lucanus, but later freed when the man became impressed with his intelligence and abilities. Terence went on to become a comedic playwright to whom many famous quotations are attributed.

Terence's plays began being performed in Rome sometime around 170 BCE. Like many Roman playwrights of his time, he adapted Greek plays to be performed before Roman audiences. Terence wrote six plays, all of which have survived in their complete form. Sometime around his twenty-fifth birthday, he would leave Rome, never to return. He may have traveled to Greece or returned to his native Carthage.

The fact that his plays were not lost, and that they were written in a simple, conversational style of writing made his plays very popular during the Middle Ages. In spite of the fact that his plays sometimes discussed subjects that were taboo or even heretical, the quality of his writing allowed his plays to escape the censure of the Church.

Terence's plays cover love triangles, dysfunctional family dynamics, and long-lost friends; one is written in part as a rebuke to Terence's critics. His popularity during the Middle Ages and after made him very influential during the neoclassical period of the eighteenth century. Thornton Wilder, a twentieth-century American writer, based his novel *The Woman of Andros* on Terence's play *Andria*.

Terence is considered a giant of Western literature due to his influence, and is often celebrated as the first poet of the African Diaspora in the West.

More Quotes From Terence

"Obsequiousness begets friends, truth hatred."

"Lovers' rows make love whole again."

"I am human, therefore nothing relating to humanity is outside of my concern."

"Time heals all wounds."

"Extreme law is often extreme injustice."

"There is nothing so easy but that it becomes difficult when you do it reluctantly."

"While there's life, there's hope."

"Nothing has yet been said that's not been said before."

"What a difference there is between a wise person and a fool!"

"There are vicissitudes in all things."

"Fortune favors the brave."

"There are as many opinions as there are people: everyone has their own way of doing things."

> *One man's religion neither harms nor helps another man.*
>
> —Tertullian

Tertullian

Tertullian is one of the most important figures in the early history of Christian literature. Born Quintus Septimius Florens Tertullianus in Carthage in 155 CE, he wrote the first major body of Latin Christian literature. Having converted to Christianity around 197, he defended the early Christian church in over a dozen

volumes of work and is considered by many to be the founder of Western Christian theology.

Tertullian is credited for being the first Latin writer to discuss the concept of the trinity, although he disagreed with contemporary doctrine regarding the Father, Son, and Holy Spirit being a single entity, instead considering them to be a group of three entities. He argued that each soul was created by God, rather than preexistent as Plato had stated. From this assertion, he concluded that the soul is naturally sinful but has within it the seeds of goodness. When this goodness awakens, he taught, the soul will naturally seek out God.

One of Tertullian's major teachings concerned whether Jesus was a man or a corporeal manifestation of the Holy Spirit. He argued that while Jesus did have a material existence, he was nevertheless a spirit, made out of nothing by the Word of God. This teaching would eventually be incorporated the Nicene Creed, which codified the theology and liturgy of the early Church.

Around 207 Tertullian apparently split with the Roman Church, and followed a Christian sect called Montanism, which believed in revelations that were not approved of by Rome. Despite this, he continued to write polemics against Gnostic theology and went on to be the predecessor of St Augustine. Tertullian died sometime after 225.

More Quotes From Tertullian

"Man is one name belonging to every nation upon earth. In them all is one soul though many tongues. Every country has its own language, yet the subjects of which the untutored soul speaks are the same everywhere."

"Truth does not blush."

"Why lean upon a blind guide, if you have eyes of your own?"

"It is certain because it is impossible."

> *Sisters, I ain't clear what you be after. If women want any rights more than they's got, why don't they just take them, and not be talking about it?*

—Sojourner Truth

Truth, Sojourner

Sojourner Truth was an abolitionist, feminist and social reform activist.

Sojourner Truth was born Isabella Baumfree in New York circa 1797. Like her parents, she was enslaved, and when she was nine years old, Isabella was sold at auction, separating her from her family. She would be sold two more times before she escaped to freedom in 1826. New York emancipated slaves on July 4, 1827. When she learned that her five-year-old son had been illegally sold to a slave owner in Alabama, she sued him and won her son's freedom. This was the first time a black woman had successfully sued a white man in an American court.

In 1843 she changed her name to Sojourner Truth, became a Methodist, and began working for the cause of abolition. She lived in a community of abolitionists in Massachusetts, where she met leaders such as William Lloyd Garrison and Frederick Douglass. In 1850 she published *The Narrative of Sojourner Truth: A Northern Slave*. She began touring and giving speeches on slavery. In May 1851, while speaking at the Ohio Women's Rights Convention, she delivered the speech for which she would become famous. The speech was published in the *Anti-Slavery Bugle* and widely distributed.

Truth continued to work for equal rights for women and African-Americans her entire life. She died on November 26, 1883, and is buried near her home in Battle Creek, Michigan.

The best way to cheer yourself is to try to cheer someone else up.

Mark Twain

Twain, Mark

Mark Twain's unique view of the world, uncanny way with words, and ability to connect with readers helped him become America's greatest literary treasure. Many of his sayings join his many brilliant works as true fabric of the nation's lexicon.

The son of a judge, Samuel Langhorne Clemens was born in the tiny town of Florida, Missouri, in 1835. The family moved east to Hannibal four years later, and its spot along the Mississippi River would shape Samuel's life and career in immeasurable ways.

Poor health kept the young Clemens indoors for much of his childhood. After his father died of pneumonia, however, a thirteen-year-old Samuel left school to become an apprentice to a printer. Two years later, he joined his brother Orion's newspaper as a printer and editorial assistant. Words already fascinated him, and he was about to embark on a journey that no one could have predicted.

That journey, of course, involved the mighty Mississippi. Clemens took a printer's job in St. Louis at age seventeen and also picked up work as a river pilot's apprentice. Soon he earned his own river pilot's license and experienced the world like he never had before. His pen name, Mark Twain, was derived from a boating expression meaning "safe to navigate." That pen name became the most famous in the history of American writers.

The 'Great American Novel'

The Civil War crippled the river trade beginning in 1861, so Twain went to work as a newspaper reporter. He was witty and wise, cranking out copy that made him a favorite read among the local audiences. When his short story "The Celebrated Jumping Frog of Calaveras County" reached the pages of the *New York Saturday Press* in 1865, Twain gained an almost immediate level of national and even international fame.

It was no fluke. Twain had a gift. He could be funny, poignant, or serious, sometimes all at once, and he did so while relating some of the most captivating stories ever told. They were stories about rather ordinary people, in tales frequently set along the Mississippi River.

His first book, *The Innocents Abroad*, was actually a collection of travel letters published in 1869. It was on that trip that he met Charles Langdon, whose sister Twain wound up marrying the following year. He and Olivia Langdon had four children.

Twain then changed the American literature landscape for good with *The Adventures of Tom Sawyer* in 1876 and *The Adventures of Huckleberry Finn* in 1885, stories about boys growing up on the Mississippi. The latter has been called the "Great American Novel." Characters like Tom, Huck, Jim, Becky Thatcher and Injun Joe became part of the American childhood experience, and remain so almost 150 years later.

In addition to the classics among his twenty-eight books and numerous short stories, essays, and letters, Twain is renowned for even smaller-sized nuggets of wisdom and wit in the form of quotes and sayings that have stood the test of time. His quips range from comical to political to societal, but they almost always carry a resonating piece of truth about life.

Though Twain died in 1910 and has no direct living descendants, his contributions to literature and Americana keep him relevant to this day. His childhood home in Hannibal is a museum, and many of the places he lived and wrote throughout the country have monuments or tributes in his honor.

More Quotes From Mark Twain

"I haven't a particle of confidence in a man who has no redeeming petty vices whatsoever."

"Soap and education are not as sudden as a massacre, but they are more deadly in the long run."

"Barring that natural expression of villainy which we all have, the man looked honest enough."

"A baby is an inestimable blessing and bother."

"All you need in this life is ignorance and confidence, and then Success is sure."

"Weather is a literary specialty, and no untrained hand can turn out a good article on it."

"A round man cannot be expected to fit in a square hole right away. He must have time to modify his shape."

"He had only one vanity; he thought he could give advice better than any other person."

"Work consists of whatever a body is OBLIGED to do, and ... Play consists of whatever a body is not obliged to do."

"Many a small thing has been made large by the right kind of advertising."

> *It is as fatal as it is cowardly to blink facts because they are not to our taste.*

John Tyndall

Tyndall, John

John Tyndall's discoveries—of the Greenhouse Effect, magnetism, and more—are still applicable today, and he was a tireless promoter of the cause of science.

John Tyndall was born in County Carlow, Ireland, on August 2, 1820. His family was poor, but he was able to have a basic education, and pursued a career as a surveyor following his schooling. In 1847, after performing surveys of England and Ireland for eight years, he became interested in the sciences. Tyndall had saved enough money from his work to be able to afford to attend the University of Marburg, Germany, from 1848 to 1850, earning a Ph.D. there. After he earned his degree, however, he had difficulty finding work for the first few years, until he was able to secure a position in 1853 at the Royal Institution in London as a professor of natural philosophy.

Scientific Study

Tyndall began studying magnetism and magnetic polarity, and pursued this research until 1856. His work on magnetism attracted the attention of other physicists of the day, and in 1852 he was inducted as a Fellow of the Royal Society. While he was at the Royal Institution, he became friends with the brilliant physicist and chemist Michael Faraday. Faraday was already extremely popular because of his entertaining and enlightening lectures. Tyndall would eventually be appointed to the chair held by Faraday upon his mentor's retirement.

Faraday had encouraged Tyndall in his successful study of magnetism, but in the late 1850s, the protégé would embark on his own area of novel research: the effects of heat and light energy (called radiant energy) on vapors and gases in the air. He was able to show experimentally that the heat in the Earth's atmosphere was caused by the ability of the gases present in the air to absorb radiant energy. He invented a device called a thermopile that converted radiant energy to electricity, which allowed him to make accurate measurements of air temperature when various gases were present. He correctly measured the radiant energy absorption potential of several atmospheric gases in 1859. His work was the first to prove the existence of the Greenhouse Effect.

In order to make his measurements as accurate as possible, Tyndall needed to ensure that there were no microscopic dust particles present in the air sample he was measuring. In the 1860s he hit upon the idea of shining intense light at the air sample; if dust particles were present, the light would be scattered. This effect, which he first described, is now called Tyndall Scattering. His work led to many other discoveries that are still relevant: in 1862 he determined a means of measuring the amount of carbon dioxide in a patient's breath, and this is still used to monitor anesthetized patients in hospitals today.

Science Education

Tyndall was also a dedicated promoter of scientific inquiry. He regularly gave public lectures on scientific topics to lay audiences at the Royal Society. On a tour of the United States, during which he delivered dozens of lectures, he was praised for his ability to not only teach science accurately, but in a manner that made it entertaining and captivated his audiences.

He wrote multiple books on science, and eventually grew to be one of the most famous physicists of his day. He often wrote and spoke about the importance of science education and how teaching was the noblest profession he could think of. He was a vocal supporter of Darwin's theory of Natural Selection, and worked against the influence of religion on science.

Tyndall died on December 4, 1893.

More Quotes From John Tyndall

"Knowledge once gained casts a faint light beyond its own immediate boundaries."

"Life is a wave, which in no two consecutive moments of its existence is composed of the same particles."

"The brightest flashes in the world of thought are incomplete until they have been proved to have their counterparts in the world of fact."

"Superstition may be defined as constructive religion which has grown incongruous with intelligence."

"We who have been born into a settled state of things can hardly realise the commotion out of which this tranquillity has emerged."

"Discussion, therefore, is one of the motive powers of life, and, as such, is not to be deprecated."

> *There are two ways of spreading light: to be the candle or the mirror that reflects it.*
>
> Edith Wharton

Wharton, Edith

Edith Wharton's ironic fiction about New York's high society that depicted the complex struggle of the individual within class constraints earned her a Pulitzer Prize in 1921 for her novel *The Age of Innocence*.

Edith Wharton (née Newbold) was born in New York City on January 24, 1862, to a family of old-money business elites. She was raised among the aristocracy of the City, and became familiar with its strict etiquette, snobbery and social taboos. She was educated at home by tutors. Her father had a large library, and Wharton read extensively. She began writing at a young age, and her poetry was noticed by Henry Wadsworth Longfellow, who recommended her parents allow her to publish it in *The New Atlantic*. Wharton completed her first novella, *Fast and Loose*, when she was sixteen. It was the first of many novels that perceptively mocked the manners of high society.

Literary Career

Edith married Edward Wharton, a wealthy Bostonian, in 1885. The couple lived on his inherited income, and traveled regularly to Europe. She continued publishing short stories in *Scribner's Magazine*, and two more novels, *The Valley of Decision* in 1902 and *The House of Mirth* in 1905.

The quote above also dates to that time period; in 1902, Wharton's long poem "Vesalius in Zante (1564)," which contains those lines, was published in *North American Review*. The

Vesalius of the title was an anatomist and physician; he died on the Greek island on Zante in 1564.

The couple moved to France in 1907, where Wharton wrote *Ethan Frome*, one of her most celebrated novels, published in 1911. It is her only novel set in the countryside, and is loosely based on real events. As her reputation increased, she and Edward, who were never close, grew apart; his mental health deteriorated and they would eventually divorce in 1913. She continued to visit the United States, but would live in France for the rest of her life.

During World War I, Wharton was instrumental in establishing organizations to support refugees from the war. She also visited the war front on several occasions to distribute medical supplies, and wrote a number of essays that urged Americans to support the Allied war effort. The essays were published in *Fighting France from Dunkerque to Belfort* in 1915. She continued to do charitable work for war survivors and homeless in France in the years following the war.

Winner of the Pulitzer Prize for Fiction

Wharton wrote *The Age of Innocence* as a four-part serial in *Pictoral Magazine* in 1920. She became the first woman to be awarded the Pulitzer Prize for Fiction for the book. *Innocence* is set during the Gilded Age among the New York aristocracy, and subtly contrasts the extreme attention to outward manners and etiquette with the hidden social machinations among that class. It also contrasted the "old" world (before WWI) with the "new." The novel was published to universal acclaim in the United States and Europe. She received an honorary doctorate from Yale University in 1923.

In 1934 Wharton published her autobiography, *A Backward Glance*. She spent her later years living at Le Pavillon Colombe in northern France, where she continued to visit with many of the noted literary figures of the day. An extraordinarily prolific writer, she penned a total of sixteen novels, sixteen short story collections, eleven non-fiction books, six novellas and three books of poetry. Her novels have been adapted more than a dozen times into films and theatre productions. Wharton died in Hyeres, France, on August 11, 1937, and was buried at Versailles.

More Quotes From Edith Wharton

"It was part of her discernment to be aware that life is the only real counselor, that wisdom unfiltered through personal experience does not become a part of the moral tissues."

"The only way not to think about money is to have a great deal of it."

"Life is always a tightrope or a feather bed. Give me the tightrope."

"The worst of doing one's duty was that it apparently unfitted one for doing anything else."

"*Life is far too important a thing ever to talk seriously about it.*"

Oscar Wilde

Wilde, Oscar

Had Oscar Wilde written only the novel *The Picture of Dorian Gray*, he would be remembered as one of Ireland's all-time greats. The full breadth of his contributions to literature and life—even its terrible turns—makes him one of the most important writers in modern history.

With a name like Oscar Fingal O'Flahertie Wills Wilde, it's no wonder he stands as one of the most famous Irishmen to ever walk the earth. And what a walk it was. In addition to providing the world some of its great plays, poems, and memorable nuggets of wisdom, Wilde lived tragedy that defines him as one of literature's most sympathetic figures.

Wilde was born in Dublin in 1854, at the site where Trinity College's Oscar Wilde Centre now sits. His mother, of Italian descent, was a lifelong Irish nationalist who wrote poetry under the pen name "Speranza," meaning "Hope" in Italian. Wilde's father was a successful ear and eye surgeon who was knighted when Oscar was ten.

It was evident early that Wilde had greatness within him. He won a scholarship at Trinity, one of the most prestigious classical schools in the world, and finished atop his class in his first year. He earned the university's highest honor in Greek, which he had been studying for nearly a decade, and then landed a scholarship to attend Oxford.

Wilde became involved in two controversial movements while at Oxford: aesthetics and the decadent movement, which favored creativity over logic and societal standards. He wore his hair long, dressed lavishly, and decorated his rooms with blue china and peacock feathers, among other accoutrements.

Wilde was harassed by fellow students at times, once even attacked by a group of them. He also earned a rustication—a temporary suspension—for nonchalantly arriving late one semester upon his return from Greece with a professor.

Launching a Career

Wilde was taking Oxford by storm when his father died in 1876, leaving the family in a financial bind. Oscar's poem, "Ravenna," had won the prestigious Newdigate prize and earned him high honors at the school. He published his first collection, *Poems*, in 1881, and in December that year he set sail for New York to deliver a series of lectures on aesthetics. The lecture circuit lasted the better part of a year and gave Wilde an audience with the likes of Henry Longfellow and Walt Whitman.

Wilde's plays, poems, and prose were gaining a considerable following. After marrying Constance Lloyd in 1884, he established himself as a successful playwright with the likes of *A Woman of No Importance, An Ideal Husband* and *The Importance of Being Earnest*. His one and only novel, *The Picture of Dorian Gray*, created a firestorm of controversy when it appeared for the first time in an American magazine in 1890. Its homoerotic themes, which would later come to be used against him at trial, were considered immoral and reprehensible by some.

It was published as a novel in 1891. That summer, Wilde began a relationship with Oxford undergraduate Lord Alfred Douglas.

Four years later, Wilde attempted to sue his lover's father for libel over the accusation of homosexuality. Oscar decided to withdraw the suit, but he was arrested himself, convicted of gross indecency and sentenced to two years of hard labor.

"The Ballad of Reading Gaol," published between Wilde's release and the death of his wife in 1898, recounted the terror of his time as a prisoner. Wilde wandered Europe in his final years, contracted meningitis, and died in 1900. Numerous biographies have been written about his brilliant, eccentric life.

More Quotes From Oscar Wilde

"A thing is not necessarily true because a man dies for it."

"Consistency is the last refuge of the unimaginative."

"A poet can survive everything but a misprint."

"And, after all, what is a fashion? From the artistic point of view, it is usually a form of ugliness so intolerable that we have to alter it every six months."

"All charming people, I fancy, are spoiled. It is the secret of their attraction."

"All art is immoral."

"People who count their chickens before they are hatched act very wisely because chickens run about so absurdly that it's impossible to count them accurately."

> *Virtue can only flourish amongst equals.*
> —Mary Wollstonecraft

Wollstonecraft, Mary

Mary Wollstonecraft was an eighteenth-century English educator and writer whose book *A Vindication of the Rights of Woman* was one of the first feminist philosophical works.

Mary Wollstonecraft was born in London on April 27, 1759. Her father was abusive, and following her mother's death in 1780, she left home and established a school for women with her sister and her best friend. In 1787 she wrote *Thoughts on the Education of Daughters* based on her experiences at the school. After working as a governess in Ireland for a few years, she returned to London and began working with Joseph Johnson, who published socially progressive texts. She began contributing to Johnson's radical political journal the *Analytical Review* in 1788.

In 1792 Wollstonecraft published *A Vindication of the Rights of Woman*, which argued that women were not inferior to men, but merely appeared so because they were systematically denied educational opportunities. She argued that educational reform would liberate women from their confined existence and argued that they should be given the same access to education as men. These ideas were revolutionary for their time, and sparked a great deal of controversy. The work was generally well received by critics and was published in America and translated into French. Wollstonecraft also wrote the feminist novel *Maria: or the Wrongs of Woman* which her husband William Godwin published after her death. The novel criticized the institution of marriage as patriarchal and oppressive, and celebrated female sexuality. Wollstonecraft died on September 10, 1797, after giving birth to her daughter Mary, who as Mary Shelley would write the novel *Frankenstein*.

More Quotes From Mary Wollstonecraft

"Independence I have long considered as the grand blessing of life, the basis of every virtue; and independence I will ever secure by contracting my wants, though I were to live on a barren heath."

"Taught from their infancy that beauty is woman's sceptre, the mind shapes itself to the body, and roaming round its gilt cage, only seeks to adorn its prison."

"It is justice, not charity, that is wanting in the world."

> *Pictures deface walls oftener than they decorate them.*
>
> — Frank Lloyd Wright

266 • Wright, Frank Lloyd

Wright, Frank Lloyd

That quote is attributed to Wisconsin native Frank Lloyd Wright, perhaps the greatest and most influential American architect of all time. In a life that spanned more than ninety-two years, Wright would experience paramount professional and creative success and satisfaction. He would also endure horrific personal heartache and strife.

The Student Becomes the Master

In Richland Center, Wisconsin, Frank *Lincoln* Wright was born on June 8, 1867; he later changed his middle name after his parents divorced. Frank studied engineering at the University of Wisconsin-Madison for two semesters before moving to Chicago to try his hand at architecture.

After six years of absorbing the style and lessons of his mentor, architect Louis Sullivan, Frank embarked on his own path. Early in his career he and his wife Catherine lived in Oak Park, a suburb of Chicago, where he built a studio adjacent to their home. During his Oak Park studio days, he worked on more than 125 commissions and developed into a supremely confident visionary. Frank championed an open concept style of "prairie" homes, characterized by their low, horizontal lines. Some of his designs from that period included the Avery Coonley house, the Darwin Martin house, the Ward Willits house, and the Robie house.

Some of his early non-residential masterpieces included the Larkin Building in Buffalo, New York, and the Unity Temple in Oak Park. He became a strong proponent for "organic architecture" in which a building's design flows cohesively with the nature around it.

Adultery! Exile!

Frank was master of his professional domain, but his domestic life was decidedly messy. Though married with enough children to fill ... well, a house ... Wright fell in love with the wife of a client for whom he was designing a home. The society that had praised and admired the architect now condemned him as an adulterer. Shunned by those around them, Frank and his mistress Mamah Cheney ditched their families in 1909 and fled to Europe.

When the lovers returned to America more than a year later, they settled down in Spring Green, Wisconsin, where Frank had spent childhood summers with relatives. There Frank designed a retreat so the couple could live away from the judgment and gossip of others. He built his famous Taliesin home on a hill overlooking the valley of the Wisconsin River.

Unfortunately, Taliesin would not prove to be the sanctuary that Frank had intended. Tragedy struck in 1914 while Frank was in Chicago overseeing a construction project. Julian Carlton, a disgruntled former servant, set fire to Taliesin. Mamah, her two visiting children, and four others tried to escape the flames, but an ax-wielding Julian blocked the only exit. He murdered seven people that day. This event devastated Frank's world.

Haunted! Cursed!

Haunted by his loss, Frank threw himself into his work, completing the Midway Garden commission in Chicago and spending several years in Tokyo, building the impressive Imperial Hotel. When the Great Kanto Earthquake of 1923 ravaged Tokyo, Frank's Imperial Hotel was one of the few buildings left standing. He also took comfort in the arms of sculptor, and alleged morphine addict, Miriam Noel. She resided with him at the newly built Taliesin II.

Frank's legal wife Catherine finally granted him a divorce in 1922, and the next year he engaged in an ill-advised marriage to Miriam. She left him by 1924. While still married to Miriam, Frank became enamored with Olga (Olgivanna) Milanoff Hinzenberg, a ballet dancer thirty-three years his junior. In another juicy scandal, Olgivanna and her daughter Svetlana dashed overseas to be with Frank at Taliesin. Her Russian architect hubby tried to have Frank arrested in violation of the Mann Act (a law that banned trafficking women across state lines), but the charges didn't stick.

In 1925 Olgivanna gave birth out of wedlock to Frank's seventh child. That same year, the Taliesin home fell victim to a second fire, this time an accident. Rumors ignited that Frank and the home were cursed.

Rebuilding a Life

The resilient architect finally married his live-in love Olgivanna on August 25, 1928. He rebuilt Taliesin a third time. Taliesin III, deemed a National Historic Landmark in 1976, still stands today. It is open for public tours and has been described as Wright's "auto-biography in wood and stone."

The next several decades would be highlighted by some of Wright's greatest professional triumphs. This included the machine-inspired and beautifully curved Administration Building of the S. C. Johnson & Son Company in Racine, Wisconsin. There were also his less flashy Usonian houses for the middle class. He designed his Fallingwater masterpiece, a breathtaking house built on a waterfall, and it graced the cover of *Time* magazine in 1938. And in 1943, he was commissioned to design the Guggenheim Museum. Throughout his life, Frank traveled tirelessly, and his designs live on all over the world, but Wisconsin was always central to his heart.

More Quotes From Frank Lloyd Wright

"Early in life I had to choose between honest arrogance and hypocritical humility. I chose the former and have seen no reason to change."

"The longer I live, the more beautiful life becomes."

"I believe in God, only I spell it Nature."

"Form follows function—that has been misunderstood. Form and function should be one, joined in a spiritual union."

"Every great architect is—necessarily—a great poet. He must be a great original interpreter of his time, his day, his age."

> *Things which seemed reasonable were often found to be untrue, and things which seemed unreasonable were sometimes true.*
>
> Wilbur Wright

Wright, Wilbur

Lifelong innovators, Orville and Wilbur Wright ushered the human race into the age of flight in 1903. Less than seventy years later, we would land on the moon.

L'Aviation en 1908. – Le Mans. – Camp d'Auvour
M. Wilbur Wright

The Wright brothers were raised in Dayton, Ohio, and were inseparable from a young age. They felt their personalities were perfectly complimentary; where Orville was an enthusiastic dreamer, Wilbur was steadier and dependable. In 1878 their

father gave the brothers a toy helicopter made of bamboo, cork and paper, and powered by a rubber band. The boys played with the helicopter until it broke, at which point they built one themselves. Years later, they would describe this episode as the beginning of their interest in powered flight. In 1892 the brothers opened a bicycle shop in Dayton. This allowed them to hone their mechanical skills and fund their interest in building a powered flying machine. In 1899 they began experimenting with aeronautics.

Kitty Hawk

In 1900 the brothers began experimenting with gliders at Kitty Hawk. They chose the location because of the strong winds that blew in from the Atlantic and the soft landings afforded by

the sandy beaches. They tested designs for powered flyers in a wind tunnel they built. By 1903 they were ready to test their first powered aircraft. On December 17, at 10:35 am, Orville piloted their propeller-driven biplane 120 feet, staying aloft for twelve seconds. They tested the plane three more times. On the last flight, Wilbur piloted the plane 852 feet in fifty-nine seconds. They continued to improve their design over the next several years, eventually securing the first contract for an airplane with the US Army. Wilbur died of typhoid in 1912. Orville retired in 1915, and spent the rest of his life serving on the board of the National Advisory Committee on Aeronautics—the forerunner of NASA.

More Quotes From Wilbur Wright

"If I were giving a young man advice in how he might succeed in life, I would say to him, pick out a good mother and father and begin life in Ohio."

"What one man can do himself directly is but little. If however he can stir up ten others to take up the task he has accomplished much."

"What is chiefly needed is skill rather than machinery."